D0614610

Lessons from China

America in the Hearts and Minds of the World's Most Important Rising Generation

Amy Werbel

Table of Contents

Acknowledgements

Lessons from China articulates my reflections on a year teaching at Guangdong University of Foreign Studies University (GDUFS) in China as a Fulbright Scholar. But if I have met my goals at all, it also is a fair reflection of the students I taught, and the colleagues and friends I worked with and learned from between August 2011 and July 2012. The names I use here for my Chinese friends are not real, because I would not want to in any way endanger their safety or privacy. Nevertheless, I hope they know how grateful I am for their cheerful patience, openness, and good company. The faculty and staff at GDUFS were models of friendliness and professionalism, and my students were a joy to teach. I learned vastly more from all of them than they possibly could have learned from me.

I am, however, happy and fortunate to share the names of the many American colleagues who helped me complete this project. Ann Bartow provided great companionship and unflagging cheer throughout our year in China, and has since remained a supportive friend. I am enormously grateful as well to two other Fulbright friends, Jill Hamburg Coplan and Patricia Mangan, with whom I have spent wonderful time in China and back at home, and who provided me with thoughtful and detailed notes on this manuscript. Visits from my dear friend Keith Pillsbury and parents Harvey and Glenda Werbel in Guangzhou relieved the homesickness we sometimes felt.

Dozens of administrators from the Council for International Exchange of Scholars, Fulbright Program, and U.S. Consulate in Guangzhou made our year abroad not only possible, but also safe and productive, including Nathan

Keltner, Victoria Augustine, Janice Englehart, Roxanne Cabral, and Timothy Guo. Nathan Keltner in particular was the bedrock support we all relied on 24 hours a day in the Mainland. He was our fixer, *par excellence* – there wasn't any problem too small or large for him to work on resolving. After I returned, Nathan contributed thoughtful advice on this text, for which I also am incredibly grateful. The professionalism and dedication of the U.S. Consulate and Embassy staff we were privileged to work with in China truly was awe-inspiring, and made me proud to represent the United States. I hope it will be clear throughout that the opinions expressed within these pages are wholly my own, and should not be interpreted in any way as expressing the beliefs, attitudes, or positions of these wonderful professionals or the Fulbright organization.

Back at home, I also am enormously grateful to my colleagues at Saint Michael's College, and especially Peter Harrigan, Susan Ouellette, Lorrie Smith, Ke-Wen Wang, and Jeffrey Trumbower. Everything I know about teaching, I learned from my colleagues and students at Saint Michael's. My year abroad relied as well on the kind support of Kathleen Adair Foster, a scholar and curator whose brilliance is matched only by her kindness and generosity. Esther Margolis provided invaluable advice on the text.

Finally, none of this would have been imaginable or remotely successful without the support and companionship of my cherished sons Graham Raubvogel and Emmett Werbel, and beloved husband Fred Lane, who came along with me for quite a ride. Graham and Meimei Zeng also provided invaluable translation, research, and assistance; I could not have written this book without their help.

This book is dedicated to all my students,
at home and abroad.

Introduction

"Surreal" is a good description of our experience
flying to Asia for the first time in early August 2011. My
older son Graham had been to China once before, but for my
younger son Emmett and I, this was by far the longest
distance we ever had traveled from home. Our journey from
Kennedy airport took us up and over the far reaches of
Canada near the North Pole, down the Eastern edge of
Siberia and Mainland China, and finally, sixteen hours later,
close to our airport hotel in Hong Kong. The next morning,
we woke up at 5 a.m. – technically dinnertime twelve hours
later at home in Vermont – and ordered dim sum in our
room. Bowls of steaming pork noodles and shrimp
dumplings arrived, along with mushy rice gruel called
congee, pickles, and tea. It was a great introduction to South
China.

A short time later, we stuffed ourselves and our small
mountain of luggage into an old-fashioned British taxi cab,
careened at a frightening pace to Hung Hom station on
Kowloon Island, and then took a short train ride to
Guangzhou, 75 miles north. And there we were, in our new
hometown, and facing our first encounter with Communist
authorities. All the paperwork recommended by the State
Department was organized neatly – original birth certificates,
my PhD diploma, health records, doctor's notes, and of
course the all-important correct and up-to-date passports with
their complicated and hard-won Z-visa residency permits.
The unflappable State Department staffer who arranged our
paperwork promised the paperwork would arrive in time, and
it did -- just as we were packing the trunk of our car to leave
for the airport on the morning of our flight.

As we waited in the line for foreigners, a scrolling digital sign loomed large behind the counter, listing the many articles and activities prohibited on the mainland, including anything that: "caused insult to Chairman Mao or the Communist party." I approached the counter with apprehension; I didn't have anything like that, but I had been warned about hassles and confiscations. Just to get the visa, I had to rush a sworn statement to Washington that I would not preach or proselytize in China, because the official in charge at the Chinese Embassy was concerned that I worked at a College with "Saint" in the title.

As it turned out, my fears were utterly unwarranted. Chinese customs and immigration officials wearing serious expressions merely checked the photos and visas in our passports, looked at our faces, and waved us through. The boys and I were now official resident aliens in the People's Republic of China. My first lesson was over – much of my fear would similarly turn out to be based on hype, rather than reality.

Despite the easy entry, our first week in Guangzhou was a trial. The early August weather was brutally hot and humid, our apartment came with beds the firmness of plywood, and we had difficulty adjusting to life with vastly less information and control than we enjoyed at home. There was no Internet or cell service on our iPhones, nobody could understand what we were saying, and we couldn't read the menus. Graham's one year of college-level Chinese saved us from total meltdown, but things were tough. And we were dazed and groggy from the twelve-hour time difference.

Our saviors in the midst of that stressful first week were a pair of adorable young men who were our first introduction to Guangdong University of Foreign Studies. Although the campus still was deserted in the first week of August, my new Dean in the Department of English

Language and Culture had kindly arranged for two skinny and bright-faced graduate students to meet us at the edge of the customs area in Guangzhou, with a small sign bearing my name. They introduced themselves as Victorious and Wonderful.

While I never quite got used to addressing them by their chosen English names, in the months ahead, I came to know and be fond of a variety of students who had chosen similarly amusing English names. Some were just old-fashioned, like May, Della, and Elsie. But others were more amusing: Pizza, Charming, Vain, Koala, Haze, and Classic. When I asked Victorious and Wonderful how they had chosen those names, they said that these were their dreams – to be "victorious" and "wonderful." Their youthful charm and optimism was a good introduction to the students who soon would take their seats in my classroom. On that hot first day though, there wasn't much opportunity for pleasant banter as the sweat dripped down our faces and soaked the backs of our shirts. We all exchanged smiles and sweaty handshakes, and then Victorious and Wonderful led us and the porters to a little bus sent from the University. In went the stuff, and off we went through the hot, crowded, and smoggy streets of Guangzhou.

The view outside the bus that first afternoon was overwhelming – a massive, sprawling city of thirteen million, with tall modern skyscrapers interspersed with streets lined with narrow shops below apartment buildings with tiny windows. Everywhere, there was laundry hanging out to dry. Victorious and Wonderful pointed out major tourist sights along the way, such as the Canton Tower, and stressed how rich the city is, as well as Guangdong Province as a whole. They both were from rural areas in Hebei, a province just north of Guangdong, and had grown up in vastly poorer conditions. They were clearly proud of what we were seeing.

From my perspective, it was a bit harder to be enthusiastic. The sky was filled with a grim and foreboding light orange fog, and the air smelled faintly like burning tires. The heat index was well over 100 degrees Fahrenheit that first day. Jet lag combined with sweat made it especially grueling to haul our heavy duffel bags to our new home on the second floor of a faculty apartment building on campus. At home it was two in the morning.

Our "V.I.P." apartment was much better than we had any reason to expect. Newly-renovated in 2010, it had foam armchairs in the living room; a small flat-screen television with 20 channels in Cantonese and Mandarin (and one English-language Communist Party propaganda channel); three small bedrooms; a kitchen with tiny refrigerator, two gas burners, and a microwave. An enclosed porch in the back held a washing machine and a pulley system for hoisting drying clothes up and down. Each room had an air conditioning unit, and after I paid the fees for the remotes and the electricity, our apartment was a comfortable oasis to which we could escape from the intense, hot, and sticky new world outside. I had heard much worse stories about housing from Fulbrighters, and I felt both relieved and a bit embarrassed about our luck to have a reasonably nice place in which to live.

That being said, this still was a major change from our two thousand square-foot house in Burlington, Vermont. Here, the three of us (soon four) would share a seven hundred square foot apartment with one small bathroom with a wall-mounted shower hose that pointed directly at the toilet. Both the shower and bathroom sinks drained through a hole in the back of the bathroom floor, which meant that you couldn't use the water too fast or the drain would back up. That would just take getting use to, but there was another major problem that required more effort to fix: when we arrived, there was nothing in the apartment besides the furniture, two flat sheets, and one pillow. Not a cup, or a towel, or any bedding at all in one of the boys' rooms. In the blizzard of our move out of our own house in Vermont, and amidst all the paperwork to get over to China, I had completely forgotten about the fact that we would have to set up house again. We soldiered on that first night, sleeping on bare, rock-hard mattresses and sharing one small hand towel in the morning for our new, combined "showlet."

Over the next few days, Victorious and Wonderful taught us how to clean our cups, bowls, and chopsticks Cantonese-style with the first pot of tea in a restaurant, and helped us with some of the modern basics, from paying for electricity to buying cell phones and phone numbers. Unlike the United States, phone numbers in China have different prices depending on how many 4's (unlucky) or 8's (lucky) they contain – I chose a cheap number with lots of 4's after deciding that I probably was not subject to Chinese laws of good and bad luck – or at least I wasn't willing to pay to find out.

Victorious and Wonderful also showed us a supermarket a few blocks from our apartment, and we went in the next morning. Our first haul included water, a bag of rice, soy sauce, sesame oil, glasses and bowls, a rice cooker, a few sheets and towels, and later on we went back for some clip-on desk lamps, batteries, light bulbs and cleaning supplies.

The supermarket for the most part was an enormous puzzle. Some things are just obvious – a bucket, broom, and sponge are basically the same wherever you go. But we had to guess what many things were on the basis of the packaging. There were lots of clues – screaming bright colors and pictures of fruits and objects announced some things we could recognize, like dishwashing liquid with a picture of a lemon and a plate. Occasionally there were even a few English words to guide us. The Arm and Hammer logo was paired with "Mr. Muscle," and "Tide" was still clearly laundry detergent, even eight thousand miles from home. But overall, there were almost no American products on the shelves, and nobody in the market spoke any English.

Unfortunately, some of what we bought in that first blur was very poor quality: itchy sheets that were too small to tuck in, a lamp that wouldn't turn on, batteries DOA, thin towels that produced vast quantities of lint but didn't actually absorb much moisture, and so on. I was hitting my first moment of cultural resistance. The stuff was ridiculously cheap, but it wasn't the level of functionality and comfort I was used to. It raised a basic question: *How Chinese was I willing to be?*

A breakthrough – or perhaps, more aptly, a breakdown on this front – came two day after our arrival, when I took Emmett to his new school across town. The American International School of Guangzhou is a massive, swanky fortress in a new part of the city called "Science Park." Close to the headquarters of major Western corporations, it serves the children of diplomats, executives, and wealthy Chinese whose children hold foreign passports. We were there to drop off Emmett's laptop to be reformatted for the school's 1:1 laptop program, and the principal happened to be in the office to greet us. When we mentioned our task of setting up the apartment, she responded like a good American ex-pat and recommended that we head to the Ikea near the train station we had arrived at. *Ikea? In Guangzhou? Really?* We went back to the apartment, and planned our trip for the next day, after Emmett and I finished the school orientation. Going anywhere involved a lot of planning, most of it relying on Graham's ability to write down addresses for us in Chinese characters taken from the

Internet, that taxi drivers could decipher. It was clear that his grasp of the language was going to have to grow quickly.

Ikea in downtown Guangzhou is exactly the same as Ikea every place else . . . except that this one is filled with Chinese people, and I do mean FILLED. As in wall-to-wall packed with young Chinese couples stuffing their baskets with things large and small, including all the semi-useless stuff you don't see in Chinese neighborhood markets – organizing bins for things that could go in free cardboard boxes, plastic kid furniture they will soon grow out of, and banal decorative wall hangings. In the lighting section, a video ran on a loop, with a perky voice discussing in British-inflected English how to buy and arrange lighting to create the appearance of "depth" in your living room. Nobody was watching – it didn't seem like anybody spoke English anyway. But they were buying the fancy lighting.

The three of us filled our two baskets with soft sheets and thick towels, light cotton blankets, foam pillows, plates, silverware, cookware, and utensils. We tried to eliminate any extraneous purchases, especially because we had to carry everything back from the gates of the University– but we still ended up with a $400.00 bill and more than 100 pounds of stuff. The most unnecessary source of weight was tucked in the bottom of one of our big blue bags -- a small stovetop coffeemaker, nestled against a couple of foil bags of the sacred beans, ground and ready to alleviate my withdrawal symptoms. At that moment, I couldn't remember why I ever thought of giving up coffee for Chinese tea. That was simply not going to work.

After three days of eating only Asian food, it was a strange experience to eat in the cafeteria at Ikea. Here, too, the cramped space was packed with Chinese couples, families, and groups of young friends lined up to fill their plates with meatballs, stuffed salmon, and mashed potatoes with gravy. Huge signs throughout the café, in English and Mandarin, told everyone how to behave. "Take a Tray Here and Put the Food on It!" "Take a Glass for Soda and a Mug for Coffee or Tea!" There were also a series of posters explaining why people should behave in this abnormal manner – why they should take their own food, why they should clear their own tray, etc.

We finally nabbed seats and sat down across from a grandmother and her son. I couldn't help staring at his shirt. It said: "Enjoy the Good Life!" and underneath were clip art pictures of soda bottles and junk food – the kind of pictures that are most often used on what-not-to-eat nutritional posters in America, crossed out with ominous black x-marks. He was pushing the meatballs on his plate back and forth with a fork awkwardly – they were covered in congealed brown gravy streaked with the white mashed potatoes. By Chinese standards, this was hideous food, and he didn't know how to hold the fork. The shirt made me worried that foreign influence would result in future generations with eating habits as bad as ours, but it probably didn't signify much of anything. Over the course of the next year, I would have many such encounters with tee-shirts sporting preposterous English phrases and logos, usually misspelled and badly rendered. Like the video loop in the lighting department, no one was paying attention – the lighting and the letters both simply signified modernity and rising class status.

Graham and I spent the first few weeks getting the apartment set up, technology straightened out, etc., while Emmett went off each morning to his swanky new International school, in the back seat of a private car we had to hire to take him back and forth. During those weeks before the semester started, I had a bit of time to wander around our new neighborhood, and immediately was impressed by the many restaurants nearby serving delicious food at unbelievably cheap prices. A Muslim family from Northwest China, for instance, offered brimming plates of fresh noodles, beef and vegetables for the equivalent of 1 dollar. Their son spent all day in the glass-walled kitchen, adding water to flour by hand, and kneading, pulling and pounding each batch of noodles to order. His biceps were enormous. A fancy dinner for three with roast goose, elegant tea service, broiled oysters, succulent pork, and vegetables ranged up to 20 dollars for three of us on a steep night. And everything was so fresh. We always had to pick out the live, swimming fish that would meet its doom for our dinner. I quickly learned that in Guangzhou, at the end of even the most horrible day, there was always astonishing food. By the end of our first month, my head had cleared just enough to be able to reflect on the tumult of events that had landed us in this remarkable new environment.

The Path to China

Boston is a tough place to schedule an architectural walking tour in April; sleet, snow, freezing rain, howling winds, and blazing sunshine – in seventeen years of leading field trips I have seen it all. But 2011 will always be a particularly special memory for me. Standing beneath the squat columns of Quincy Market, and pointing across the crowds to the Neo-classical elements of Faneuil Hall, I felt the buzz of an incoming text message on the cellphone in my pocket. I was pretty sure I knew who was buzzing. I quickly sent my eleven undergraduate students off for an early lunch break, towards pizza and chowder, and headed inside the market a bit further to escape the cold breeze. My husband Fred and I had arranged that he would text me if a letter arrived from the Fulbright Board at our mailbox in Vermont while I was gone. I had been designated a finalist in the

China competition in November, and knew that announcements were due any day. His text on that cold, clear April day was concise: "Fulbright letter!!"

My correspondent, the Fulbright Scholarship Board, was the brainchild of a towering figure in the history of United States legislators. In 1946, Senator J. William Fulbright surveyed the devastated post-World War II global landscape, and launched what is today the world's most prestigious cultural exchange program. Among his core beliefs was the idea that regular and ongoing intellectual exchange would "continue the process of humanizing mankind to the point, we would hope, that men can learn to live in peace--eventually even to cooperate in constructive activities rather than compete in a mindless contest of mutual destruction." President Harry Truman signed legislation creating the Fulbright program in the following year.

Over the course of the past sixty years, Senator Fulbright's words have inspired the more than three hundred thousand professors, students, and researchers around the world who have taken part in the program. As it turns out, the thin letter in Fred's hands carried good news. Although I can't claim to have ended the world's "mindless contests" during my time abroad, I certainly did achieve several of the Senator's smaller goals, including acquiring greater "empathy – the ability to see the world as others see it, and to allow for the possibility that others may see something we have failed to see, or may see it more accurately." My biggest lesson this past year was that we have at least as much to learn about improving ourselves from studying China, as they have to learn about improving themselves from studying us.

I submitted an application for a Fulbright to teach American Studies in China in August, 2010, for a slot in the program beginning the following year. Then I waited, and waited, as my application ricocheted back and forth between Washington, D.C. and Beijing. The process for selecting and placing China Fulbrighters is exceptionally lengthy, as the program seeks input by many different parties. The whole process starts with the Council for International Exchange of Scholars in Washington, followed by intense reviews in China, led by the Education office at the U.S. Embassy in Beijing. Finally, the Fulbright Scholarship Board back in Washington makes a final decision. As a result of all the paper shuffling, we didn't find out where we were going until early June. When the process sugared-off (as we like to say in maple-syrup soaked Vermont), we found out that my family would be sent to Guangzhou, the largest city in South China, where I would teach at Guangdong University of Foreign Studies.

My package of benefits included travel money for myself and both my boys, housing, salary replacement for the year, a book allowance, private school tuition for Emmett (going into 8th grade), and a travel health policy for each of us that among other things, promised medical helicopter evacuation and even "return of remains" if necessary. Today, the Fulbright program in China is larger, and more generous, than the Fulbright posts in any other country in the world, with contributions from State Department funds, major donors, as well as the Chinese government.

The history and recent expansion of the Fulbright program in China reflects both massive shifts in the nation's fortunes, as well as in the strategic importance of its current relationship with the United States. Although Chinese government officials under the Nationalist administration were among the first to sign on with the Fulbright program in 1947, the arrangement only lasted two years. In 1949, the Communist Party of China (CPC) seized power and launched a new nation – the People's Republic of China (PRC) – under the charismatic leadership of Mao Zedong. The early years of the PRC were not promising for those seeking to bring cultural exchange to China, as Mao implemented disastrous agricultural policies in the 1950s that resulted in vast scourges of famine and disease. The tumultuous and tragic Cultural Revolution that followed from 1966 to 1976 only increased the nation's global isolation.

During those horrifying years, there weren't any Fulbrighters in China. Public schools were closed or converted to ideology indoctrination centers, an entire generation of scholars was sent to the countryside to be "re-educated" as peasants, and deaths from murder and starvation are estimated in the tens of millions. The party utterly failed in its effort to purge China of its ancient religious and cultural traditions and capitalistic inclinations, but it did succeed in terrorizing and scarring a nation. It was not until 1979 – following the death of Mao and the official start of Deng Xiaoping's "Reform and Opening" movement – that Fulbrighters started trickling back into the world's most populous country again.

In the past eight years, the China program has expanded significantly, due to America's interest in forging stronger bonds with the world's most important rising power (and America's largest foreign creditor – as of June 2012, China held $1.1 trillion in U.S. Treasury securities). Clearly, the growth of the program indicates that higher-ups think it can make a positive difference. So what, exactly, was I being paid to do?

For the past seventeen years, I have led students in discussion about the history of the United States, with a special focus on visual culture: paintings, sculptures, architecture, urban and landscape planning, furniture, prints, cartoons, etc. Because I went to college and graduate school in the 1980s and 1990s, my training and teaching focus thematically on the four pillars of post-modern analysis: gender and sexuality, race and ethnicity, power and class relations, and attitudes towards nature and the environment. Translate this short list to: white male privilege, genocide against Native Americans, slavery and subsequent racist oppression, exploitation of immigrants and laborers, repression of women and homosexuals, and environmental destruction. In short, teaching American cultural history through a post-modern lens is hardly the most obvious way to promote positive feelings about the United States.

Although technically the Fulbright program is supposed to emphasize "cultural" exchange, in my year I was one of only eight American lecturers in the field of humanities, while ten others were invited to share their expertise in more practical subjects – law, journalism, health policy, economics, etc. I thought the problem of national critique was unique to my own branch of the academy, but as it turns out, many of us felt the same tension about how to discuss the realities of American life, past and present.

At our first Fulbright orientation in Washington in late June, I asked the question, and many of the other professors in the room nodded their heads: Was it advisable or expected that we sugarcoat our history a bit for our Chinese students? Maybe spend less time on the Indian Removal Act and lynching than we usually do? Surprisingly (and gratifyingly), our State Department orientation leaders were unanimous in insisting that we teach as we did at home. We were not going to China to make the United States look better than it is – but rather to share what it feels like to be in a classroom in which everyone is free to scrutinize history without fear. One of the senior officials in the room confirmed the sentiment: "Diversity of opinion is our strength. Show them that."

Those four days in Washington were the prologue to

a thoroughly fascinating year. We certainly were a diverse group: evenly mixed between men and women, assembled from all over the United States, from small colleges like mine and major research universities, some with families tagging along and others on their own. For some sessions, we met in a large hotel conference room along with the many student researchers who also were going to improve their language skills and further academic work. Speakers included State Department officials and scholars of contemporary China. For other sessions, we met in small groups just for professors, organized by discipline. Advice in these chatty sessions was much more wide-ranging: "Don't assign more than fifteen pages of reading at a time," "Say you don't drink at all or you will be forced to drink until you pass out," and "Bring your own feminine hygiene products." The State Department officials gave us just one hard and fast rule: *Never directly criticize the Communist Party, or publicly talk about Taiwan, Tienanmen Square, Tibet, or North Korea.* As I was later to discover, these are topics that abruptly end dialogue with most Chinese.

Not talking about China, North Korea, etc. was pretty easy for me, because I am in no way what people refer to as a "China hand," meaning a foreigner who has mastered the language and culture enough to really understand them. And I certainly didn't know much about South East Asian politics either. To be quite frank, I applied without thinking the whole thing through for very long. My 17-year old son Graham wanted a gap year in China before college to study Mandarin intensively, my younger son Emmett, 14 and in the 7th grade, was itching for an adventure, and I was impressed by the package of pay, benefits and of course prestige. Fred had a relatively flexible work schedule, and a similar inclination towards adventure. As an attorney, author, and computer forensics expert, he was able to come for roughly half the time, and do much of his work online from China during the months he joined us.

Almost exactly twelve months after a perhaps too-brief "do it Mom!" conversation with the boys that led to my application, I boarded a massive airplane with Graham and Emmett, as utterly stressed as I have ever been. From mid-April, 2011 when I got the good news at Quincy Market, to our departure at the beginning of August, a million things had to be arranged in a frighteningly short amount of time. Finishing my classes at Saint Michael's, enrolling the kids in new schools, medical examinations and immunizations, financial arrangements, figuring out what to do with our pets, squaring off against Rosetta Stone Mandarin, voraciously reading books like *China in the 21st Century, Everything You Need to Know*, and then, moving out of our house to make room for year-long tenants. The sixteen-hour flight to Hong Kong was the most relaxation I had experienced since reading the acceptance letter four months earlier. On many occasions, I felt simply bewildered and overwhelmed by this turn in life. Could it really be true that we were leaving our adorable, pristine city of Burlington, Vermont for a city of 13 million that is consistently ranked among the most polluted places in the world? That it all felt surreal is an understatement.

Back to School

At the end of the month, I flew to our second, weeklong Fulbright orientation in Beijing, on a spanking new Air China Airbus plane (most of the planes I boarded in China had that new-plane smell). It was time to think about teaching. What I was most curious to know was what my new students would be like. The differences undoubtedly would be dramatic.

For the past seventeen years, I have taught art history and American studies as professor at a small, Catholic liberal arts college named Saint Michael's, in Northwestern Vermont just outside of Burlington. At 40,000 residents, Burlington is the behemoth in the State. In China, it would be considered a medium-sized village – currently, Beijing has more than 20 million. So, the first major difference for me was going to be size. Guangdong University of Foreign Studies enrolls more than 20,000 students, in a complex labyrinth of departments, and sub-departments. That's a huge contrast to Saint Michael's, which offers a compact assortment of traditional liberal arts majors to about 2,200 undergraduates.

Our second State Department orientation in Beijing was impressively comprehensive, and I was extremely fortunate already to have been acclimated to my living situation. Emmett's school started early, so we had to arrive during the first week of August. But all the other professors were just arriving in China, and so the faces around the table were somewhat tired and worn.

Nevertheless, everyone was excited. Around the table were several friendly faces from Washington who soon would become dear friends and comrades in soft power arms, including Ann Bartow, a law professor from Pace University, on her way to Shanghai; Jill Hamburg Coplan, a journalist and lecturer at NYU, traveling with her two rambunctious tween sons to Beijing; Erin Ryan, a law professor from Oregon, who lucked out with placement at the beautiful seaside town of Qingdao, albeit in a claustrophobic apartment shared with her husband, small son, and mother; and Patricia Mangan, a cultural anthropologist from Smith College who would spend a frustrating year with her small daughter in the far-West city of Kunming, enduring a variety of plagues, but also in love with her devoted students. There were many more men and women I came to admire that year in our cohort, including Harry Williams, an historian headed to freezing-cold Changchun, not far from the borders of North Korea and Siberia; and Karen Meenan, a public health expert from Oregon traveling with her two daughters, who valiantly worked to gather reliable statistics on issues such as the occurrence of domestic violence in China.

Our group of eleven fall arrivals was especially lucky, as our orientation in Beijing -- near the US embassy -- was able to include far more important speakers than the mid-year meeting in Xiamen. We enjoyed a lengthy visit from the new American Ambassador to China, Gary Locke, who already was a sensation after just a few months on the job. His fame derived in large part from a photo circulated on Chinese microblogs, showing the new Ambassador buying his own coffee at an airport – something no Chinese official of similar stature would ever do. (Locke replaced Jon Huntsman, who left the post to campaign unsuccessfully for the Republican nomination for President in 2012.) Among the many things I learned that day is the protocol that everyone in the room rises when an Ambassador enters. He was so new to the job, however, that he seemed somewhat embarrassed when we adhered to tradition.

Like many of his colleagues, Ambassador Locke impressed upon us that we were part of an effort to build inter-personal relationships, which Embassy staff had little opportunity to do. We also would be expected to provide informal briefings from our posts – the students in our classrooms are of intense interest around the world, as experts struggle to predict how China's Internet generation will behave. Fulbright's vision regarding the significance of the program was still clearly shared by all the officials who spoke to us. Our work was "soft power" at its softest and yet most powerful.

For most of three days, we heard from American government officials specializing in U.S.-China relations, whose "packets" covered economics, finance, law, environment, and human rights. We learned what to tell students who wanted to study in the United States about the visa process, heard briefings on health concerns, including air, water, and food, and were warned against arguing about sports and politics in bars (as other Americans had done to ill effect before us).

The most depressing briefing (among many contenders) came from the Embassy's Human Rights officer on the Chinese legal system; among other things, he provided an overview of recent crackdowns on lawyers, writers, and other anti-government activists. The global revolutionary fever of 2011 had resulted in many steps backwards in this area of China's "reform and opening." All of this was fascinating and sobering, and I felt quite privileged to be in the room with so many intelligent, passionate, and dedicated State Department officials. But what I was really looking forward to were the days devoted to teaching, and those came at the end. The clock was ticking, classes were starting in a few days, and I had no idea what to expect.

The most memorable portion of our briefing on Chinese education was delivered by a group of exceptionally bright local students who had been gathered by State Department officials from Peking and Tsinghua Universities (sometimes called the Harvard and MIT of China). To understand Chinese students, they told us, we first would need to understand the (feared and loathed) *gaokao.*

In a country with 1.4 billion people with a history of make-it-or-break-it examinations dating back thousands of years, the *gaokao* was perhaps an inevitable and unavoidable development. Currently, roughly nine million high school seniors each year vie for seven million university slots by taking a single test, which lasts for two or three days in June (depending on the Province). This is the *gaokao*. Think of it as the SAT exam multiplied a thousand times, both because it depends on years of memorization (constituting most of high school), and because it is almost the sole determinant of a student's university placement. Students are grilled on subjects chosen from Chinese, Math, English (or another foreign language), Physics, Chemistry, Biology, History, Geography, and Political Education. Extra points are sometimes given to students with particular accomplishments, or those who are members of an identified ethnic minority, but any way you slice it, for the vast majority of Chinese students, the *gaokao* is everything.

As a result of this do-or-die system, Chinese high school students do not engage in extra-curricular activities, worry about composing cute but serious admissions essays, or contribute hours of *de rigeur* public service. One student panelist described studying for 14 hours each day. For her, there was no dating, no social life, just pure memorization. For two straight years, she took off only one afternoon each month. Another student on our orientation panel simply summarized that his "happy childhood ended with *gaokao*." He was one of the lucky few to earn a spot at Peking University, thus ensuring his future success. Students who fail to win a place in the nation's enormous higher education system are assured of a lifetime of difficult and underpaid work, in factories, fields, or even worse. Doing well requires a level of commitment, patience, and focus no American student is ever expected to master.

Although the *gaokao* is universally criticized, nearly everyone also recognizes that it has some enormous advantages as well. These play out in some academic ways, but can most easily be seen in their larger social effects. One of the student panelists remarked that "it isn't flexible, but it is fair," because students can study hard and overcome class differences. I found this to be a lesson that was both true and poignant, as so many of my Chinese students described to me brutal childhood living conditions. I heard about parents who were out of work for years, families constantly struggling to earn enough money to support elders, and scrambling to feed children a basic diet. Crowded living conditions with no heat or hot water in cold regions were common tales, as were reports of living with intermittent or no electricity.

With good grades and behavior in elementary school, these students had been plucked from impoverished villages, educated at regional boarding schools largely at government expense, and then trained exhaustively for the *gaokao* that would determine their future. They did what they were supposed to do, and for them, the system worked. The cost? -- For those with some means, a maximum of 6,000 RMB per year for tuition, room, and board at university – or roughly $1,000. And financial aid is readily available for those students who come from the poorest families. Very few students leave Chinese universities with debt, and if they do, it's tiny.

Not surprisingly (once again) this central feature of modern Chinese life was orchestrated by the ever-pragmatic and progressive Deng Xiaoping, as one of the earliest initiatives of his Reform and Opening Campaign. In 1977, officials under Deng committed themselves to rebuilding the nation's education system. They instituted the *gaokao*, reopened K-12 schools and universities and built new ones, and created thematic programs (including Guangdong University of Foreign Studies University), all the while keeping efficiencies high and costs low.

Deng clearly recognized that China's future would rest on its ability to build a middle class, and a pool of talent for operating within a competitive global marketplace. It's hard not to find the whole system at its core both idealistic and impressive, but of course, as I was to find out, there also are a lot of problems. There are important lessons for America both in the extraordinary successes and deficiencies of Chinese education.

Among the many "efficiencies" of the Chinese system is the practice of selecting students' majors and universities for them, based chiefly on the availability of slots, and the results of the *gaokao*. Provincial and National governments control the vast majority of academic institutions in China, so they can decide to create programs based on societal needs in short order, which is quite a bit different than the way such changes occur in the vastly decentralized U.S. system. Chinese students can indicate their preferences for majors and universities, but once again, the *gaokao* determines all. They take the test in June, and weeks later are offered three choices of very particular majors in specific universities they often know little about. One of our student panelists, for example, applied to study economics, which routinely yields high-paying corporate work in China. But his scores relegated him to the less-preferred domain of English Language and Culture, so he began his college career and work life in frustration and disappointment.

Many of my own students later told me similar stories. They seemed genuinely shocked when I described how my own students were often "exploratory" majors, who changed their minds several times about majors and career paths after enrolling in College. In China, switching majors is almost unheard of. One student confided to me that she hated what she was doing and just "felt lost."

The so-called "cold" (or unpopular) majors include almost all of the humanities -- history, languages, literature, etc. -- fields whose graduates do not earn especially high salaries. Cold majors also are dominated by women, several students told me, because they are considered to be more "naturally gifted" in these fields. The resultant pay and prestige gap between men and women didn't seem to be a specific concern, but nonetheless, my female students would discuss these facts with me while rolling their eyes, and in a tone of exasperation.

A more frequent complaint -- and source of ridicule – concerns the large number of political theory courses students are required to complete, which they consider to be "boring, useless, and tedious." These include: Principles of Marxism, Mao Zedong Thought and Socialism, Deng Xiaoping, and Military Training and Theory. On end-of-the-year exams, students are required to regurgitate memorized quotations from Mao, current five-year-plans, and the like. Even my graduate PhD students were required to keep taking political ideology courses – the subject was endless, and they all considered it endlessly useless. One of our student panelists in Beijing claimed that these courses functioned mainly "for making jokes with other university students." "If you can understand those jokes," he told us, "you can understand China."

Joking aside, the student panelists for the most part were serious, circumscribed, and concerned. They didn't seem as optimistic as I would have expected from students with the "best and the brightest" prospects in China, and this was another early and powerful lesson that would evolve for me over the coming months.

Back in the United States, China is portrayed as the dynamic face of the 21st Century – a nation experiencing the most rapid economic expansion ever seen in human history. Even the hyper-critical *New York Times* is filled with stories of awe-inspiring infrastructure projects, bullet trains, and impending world domination. So, why were these impressive students less than thrilled? Weeks later, one of my students summed up a typical response to this question in just three (bitterly-delivered) words: *"At what price?"* Throughout my year in China, the students I spoke with were much more pervasively pessimistic than my own students in the United States, who arguably have at least as much to worry about.

In Beijing, the students confided that they talk a lot among themselves about major concerns regarding the nation's future, including: party rule, environmental problems, and the legal system. Mostly, like my own students, they worried about their own futures. When asked, many admitted that they were members of the Party, but nobody had anything good to say about it. Joining the Party is an important career move for young Chinese, and this was equally true for my own students in Guangzhou. Party membership opened doors, and increased the chances of gaining a coveted civil service (or "iron rice bowl") job, with its many attendant perks. As one student bluntly stated, "the Government controls everything in society, so you can enter their circles, and you can have a good life." An example he gave was the important *hukou* residence permit, required to live legally in Beijing and other popular cities. Millions of migrant workers from the countryside reside in the city without one, and they are relegated to difficult lives with no access to basic services, including housing, subsidized health care, and public education for their children.

Finally, at the end of our last session with the students, one of the Fulbright professors asked the major outstanding question that was on all of our minds. What did Chinese students expect, and want, from foreign professors? One student started by sharing some common and benign views. They are curious about what goes on in foreign universities, they enjoy new styles of teaching, and they believe that most foreign teachers are popular. But another student responded in a much more personal and heartfelt manner. He started by talking about his own childhood, growing up in Southern China in a newly middle-class family. As a small boy, he said, he "watched television from Hong Kong, and there was not much pressure from school." He wanted to travel and explore the world.

But then came school, and from an early age, he was required to sit and memorize for most of the day. This, he said, is "very bad for China." This is "quite dumb." There was no time to think about what he wanted to be – only to work to pass the exam. He had no idea who he was, or what he wanted to be. Even worse, when his dream finally came true, he found that college was often the same as high school. Memorization was the key to success, and this made his classes "very boring." Many students, he said skip class because it seems useless since they can just memorize the textbook during the last two weeks before the exam.

What he most wanted from foreign professors, he said, was to learn critical thinking to help him achieve a difficult goal -- to work on human rights protection. "China must do this to be on the international stage – to put the issue on the table." First, he wanted to make money, and then "do what he wants to do" as a lawyer. Professors like us could provide not only greater interaction than they were used to, but also knowledge, and inspiration. Chinese professors were pragmatic, and always talked about lowering expectations and working within the system. He told us that foreigners often had ideas that seemed hopeless in China, but nonetheless they were inspiring.

Another student discussed similar possibilities for new thinking. In high school, she said, students only learned Marxist theories and philosophy. But her Western professor introduced other theories and this caused her to "suspect" what she learned in high school. This was a great revelation, and had opened entirely new ways of thinking about everything.

There really isn't a better summary of what we were there to do, and in fact what we should be doing as professors wherever we are, at home or abroad. Ultimately, my year in China hammered home with enormous power a lesson I already knew from seventeen years in the classroom: If you do nothing else, teach your students to think critically, and help them use education to develop into purposeful and self-aware adults. The student panel was the most important send-off to my own classroom the next week, and I took their advice to heart.

Over the course of the next year, my students and I criticized, debated, disagreed, puzzled over contradictory information, and generally interrogated American history. They asked questions about topics they were interested in that they could otherwise discuss publicly only in rare circumstances-- homosexuality, minority rights, political corruption. The history in my class was not a series of names, dates, and events to be memorized, but rather a living and subjective narrative. Many had never read primary sources in a history class before, or scholarship that had not been concocted by a group of professors under the direction of a Communist Party Secretary.

On the advice of those in Washington, and even in Guangzhou, my students and I were pretty free. What happened over the course of these fascinating months was not just that my students saw a different approach to history – a new theory -- but that I saw the history of my own country through an entirely new lens. Watching my students dig deeply into our tragic and transcendent past, in the light of their understanding of China's own tragic and transcendent past, proved to be a transformative experience for all of us.

Course One: Culture in the United States from the Civil War to World War I

From the painful legacy of slavery through the birth of our more progressive modern state, my students and I were amazed at the parallels between the era of America's emergence on the world stage, and their own present reality.

Chapter One. Teaching Slavery: Family Matters

My seminar titled "American Culture from the Civil War to World War I" met for just eighty minutes each week on Tuesday mornings, in a small and worn classroom on the first floor of Building #2. In contrast to Saint Michael's, none of the buildings here were named after people -- the only donor at GDUFS was the government, and so every building was given a number based on when it was built. Building #2 was a fairly typical sprawling classroom building, with picture-less hallways opening onto small- and medium-sized rooms. The computer, ceiling-mounted projector, and software all were American – but several versions behind my classrooms at home, and there weren't any niceties like smart boards, dimmable lights, or blackout shades. Nonetheless, when something didn't work, a student would scurry out of the classroom and return within minutes with a technology assistant who fixed the problem. What we had, on the whole, worked reliably and well. On each floor of Building #2 there was one much larger and better equipped lecture hall, but my class did not require much space – only eleven students had enrolled for credit, and another half-dozen audited on an informal basis. The course was designated as "selective," meaning not required, so only students who were genuinely interested in American culture signed up.

My graduate courses were by far the most satisfying to teach, because the students' English was generally excellent, and they were focused on and fascinated by the subject of American culture. These seminar students were all in the second year of Master's programs in English Literature and Culture. They already had majored in English as undergraduates, and now were preparing for careers as professors or high school teachers, or for unknown paths that required good translation skills. Despite the luxury of my students' rapt attention, and adequate technology, other aspects of the teaching environment were far from perfect. From my perch on a small podium at the front of the room, I looked down on my students, crammed into tiny wooden seats in immovable rows, with small desks in front of them. It was impossible for them to turn around and look at each other. There was no climate control, other than some rickety, noisy ceiling fans, and the thin window-frames barely kept out the wind and rain that sometimes howled outside.

In September and June, the class was stiflingly hot, and we had to run the noisy fans to cope with the heat. In the winter, the damp concrete held in a bone-chilling cold; everyone bundled up in coats and hats for class. The spring was perhaps most odd, as the floors, walls, and furniture were soaked with condensation. My students waded into class as though all this was perfectly normal – I didn't bother to share with them my thoughts about the cultural and economic differences at play. But it certainly did make me realize how spoiled we are in America in comparison.

In my own classrooms at home, it is always roughly 70 degrees, come ice storm or heat wave. If my students at home froze in class, they would complain loudly, and the College would scramble to fix the problem. But not so in China . . . these students clearly felt privileged just to be in class, even when it was freezing cold, or a river of condensation soaked their feet. If anything, their discomfort only bonded them more deeply to each other as friends.

All the graduate students in the Department knew

each other extremely well, and bundled into the tight rows each week elbow to elbow, even though there was plenty of room to spread out. They brought small notebooks in which they took copious notes, with pencils pulled from decorative cases. The six men all sat together in rows behind the five women. There was very little fraternizing – and no flirting – between the sexes. Throughout their education, whether undergraduate or graduate, they largely moved together within small same-sex groups, taking identical courses with others in their major, and also bunking together in the dorms. My first impression was that they were passionately eager to learn. And I had plenty to teach them.

High school students in China learn very little about American history (though definitely more than American students learn about China). This subject is covered in a broad sweep of World History, and is often lumped together with histories of other English-speaking countries. I opened a visiting lecture at a technical college in South China once by asking students what they remembered about American history, and a young woman yelled out: "Your country was founded by criminals." I knew then that we would need to cover some basics before proceeding.

In this small graduate seminar, my students definitely knew more than that young woman – they remembered the War for Independence and the Civil War, and they usually knew something about Native Americans and Westward Expansion. The subject they always remembered best, though, was slavery – probably because it most irrefutably supported the general Chinese line on America as the world superpower of hypocrisy. Criticize policy on Tibet? -- *what about slavery?* Uyghur suppression? – *how about that slavery?*

In response to a homework assignment, one of my seminar students wrote: "On one hand, America wants to

project its image to the world as the free land where everyone
is equal, but on the other hand its people can not get rid of
their bias towards people of another race." And another
student wrote: "America attracts millions of immigrants to
this 'land of free' for her inclusive society, together with the
'American Dream' that seeks for equal opportunity and
bright future. However, American society, as far as I am
concerned, is not the same as the common stereotype, but, is
still a white supremacy society. . . White people regard
themselves as the real host of the country, and other races
should be under the guidance and control of them." Needless
to say, slavery and the Civil War were subjects about which
my students were eager to learn more.

Research on slavery in the United States is an
enormously dynamic and well-developed area of study --
from the economics and politics of the global slave trade, to
the archaeological remains and cultural legacies of slaves in
individual communities throughout the Caribbean and United
States, to vibrant debates about post-colonial theory and the
potential for a post-racist society.

My own approach to teaching this subject in my
undergraduate survey course in the United States has been to
emphasize the agency of West Africans in the face of the
most severe and brutal repression imaginable. To that end, I
usually begin with one or two classes on traditional West
African philosophy, religion, and art, and then segue to the
Caribbean and Southern United States, charting the
disruptions and continuities of these traditions in the context
of slavery, as seen in burial practices, ceramics, textiles,
architectural styles, and other aspects of visual culture.

At Saint Michael's, when we approach the Civil War,
students look both at arts created by slaves, as well as images
of African-Americans by European-Americans on both sides
of the abolition debate. All along the way, I emphasize that

there are no "American" perspectives, but rather a multiplicity of points-of-view based on economic realities; status and power hierarchies; gender, race, ethnic, sexual, and cultural traditions and assumptions; as well as individual intellectual and artistic temperaments. In studying American culture, generalizations are especially useless.

For students in my undergraduate survey courses in China, all of this had to be condensed into fairly simple English, which was a painfully reductive process. My dense lectures on ancient African beliefs about death, gender, empowerment, and the importance of creative agency in those courses were reduced to bullet points like these:

- Slaves came from many diverse African communities, and spoke different languages.
- Ties of language, religion, and culture were broken, but not completely.
- Harriet Powers' quilts display African techniques and Christian symbols.

My graduate students thankfully were able to engage in much deeper conversation, and so we had the opportunity to dig into the subject of slavery much more substantially. Thanks to their thoughtfulness and excellent language skills, I was able to see this most difficult history in a new way through their eyes.

The first surprise for me was that my students had never studied American history using primary sources before. They were grateful and fascinated by the group of readings and art images I assigned them to read and write about, including works by the escaped slave and abolition crusader Frederick Douglass, the poets Walt Whitman and Emily Dickinson, the painter Winslow Homer, and sculptor Edmonia Lewis (who is half African-American and half Chippewa). I asked them each week to develop a critical question about each "text," and then to write an answer to the question that most interested them. All of this had to be e-mailed to me in advance of the class, so I could gauge how much they understood, and what interested them. Douglass' autobiography was by far the most popular choice to write about. As I was to discover, it hit a nerve deep in Chinese culture regarding the weighty significance of family ties.

Frederick Douglass' *Narrative of the Life of Frederick Douglass, An American Slave* (1845) begins with a devastating account of his childhood – and what little he knew of his family. His mother, "quite dark," was Harriet Bailey, a slave in Maryland. Although she traveled to visit her son on a few occasions during his childhood, he barely could remember her. Douglass was even less clear about his father, reputed to be a white man, and "[t]he whisper that my master was my father may or may not be true; and, true or false, it is of but little consequence [since] . . . the slaveholders have . . . by law established, that the children of slave women in all cases follow the condition of their mothers."

In keeping with another depraved but "common custom," Douglass' mother was leased to a farm a considerable distance away when Douglass was just a baby. He bitterly surmised: "for what this separation is done, I do not know. Unless it is to hinder the development of the child's affection toward its mother, and to blunt and destroy the natural affection of the mother for the child." This passage of the text was the one most often addressed by my students in their homework:

> Slave-holders took the children from their mothers in order to destroy the family affections between them. Cutting off the emotional ties among the slaves and making them alienated from each other can effectively blur the identities of the black children

who were born to be a new generation of slaves, check the healthy growth of their mentality and emotion; therefore they could make a little boy or girl into a cold working machine that knows nothing but serving its master. Without natural human affections, the enslaved people were not able to unite and resist their mighty lords. I assume this was one of the reasons that made the slave-holders do that.

Another student similarly wrote:

As far as I can concern, the separation between the children and their mothers is not only a trick that can just cut off the relationship between the two generations, but also a scheme that aims to make disappeared the cultural transmit during the development of the black ethnicity. That is more serious than the segregation or even the genocide because it avoids the cultural links, the inner spiritual essence, be instilled into the new generation. It is a dark artifice under the cover of something else to destroy the blacks.

In class, we followed up further on this important, though rather small point in a much larger story, and it struck me that they fully understood the weight of this detachment in a way that my American students and I could not. If Douglass could not acknowledge his father, know his mother, and belong to the place he was born and raised, then how could he develop fully into a human being? It was not until I visited my student Mary at her ancestral village in Foshan that I fully understood the depth of their empathy.

Like most of my students, Mary showed up to class each day on time, bunked in next to her friends in the narrow, attached, wooden seats, and paid rapt attention throughout class. Her short bob hairdo was always well-combed, and her outfits demonstrated a relatively conservative taste in fashion. I never saw her wearing the tights-and-booty-shorts combo and three-inch heeled boots that seemed to be the latest trend among many of the students. On a few occasions in the fall semester, Mary came to visit me during office hours, to chat about her progress, and practice her English skills through general conversation. Since I didn't know her especially well, I was surprised, and pleased, when she invited me to visit her family for the "Yuan Xiao Jie" or Lantern festival. Yuan Xiao Jie is celebrated on the fifteenth day of the first lunar month of the year, and marks the end of the two-week Chinese New Year celebration, as well as the students' long winter break from school.

Foshan is the type of city that Americans typically read about in grim news reports about the dark side of the "new" China. A sprawling factory town just twelve miles from Guangzhou, Foshan plays host to miles of box-like factories and warehouses, producing many of the sneakers, computers, and other consumer goods we are used to buying cheaply in America. This region of South China has been open to trade – and production – far longer than any other, and early on became a lynchpin in Reform and Opening planning as a Special Economic Zone welcoming foreign investment. The massive scale and monotonous design of Foshan's factory buildings are chilling reminders that they were not built for treasured socialist laborers -- their harsh and impersonal interior environments rather have been the target of critics, and protestors, for many years. In 2010, several thousand workers in Foshan staged a protest at a Foxconn plant over low wages and inhumane working conditions. Foshan also has been host to a lot of other protests reported in the Hong Kong and Western press as well in recent years, over government land seizures, polluting waste incinerators, and corrupt officials.   Although Foshan is famous for its manufacturing plants, its posh business district reveals no trace of the source of its new wealth. Instead, it is dominated by an entirely recent and enormous park, with a *faux* lake, canals, and walking paths surrounded by glass-walled skyscrapers – reflecting mostly bulldozers and cranes building more. Major chain hotels have begun to move in, including, most spectacularly, a massive Intercontinental at the top of the lake. In this area, there isn't a speck of litter visible on the streets, and rows of small saplings and shrubs promise one day to fill out and provide some greenery. There is not a single trace of the small farms and villages that were seized and bulldozed to make this new Foshan. The rest of the city, in contrast, sprawls into the distance with a much less cohesive veneer – like many Chinese "cities," Foshan was cobbled together from dozens of traditional small villages to make an administrative region under the Communist regime.

A brand-new train line runs between Guangzhou and Foshan as an extension of the metro, and so it didn't take me long to get to the end of the line. Coming out of the train entrance, a pod of motorcycle riders waved at me and, confused, I waved back. Mary later explained that they are a popular form of taxi in Foshan (although they are illegal in Guangzhou). I hit yet another point of cultural confusion as Mary introduced me to her father and "sister," who had come to meet me in a new high-end black Toyota sedan. The sister, dressed in jeans and a pink velour sweatshirt was actually a cousin --as Mary later explained to me, first cousins are often treated as siblings, and consider themselves as such. She was a wonderfully fun twelve-year old, eager to show off her English, and quick to roll her eyes in adolescent protest against nearly everything her Uncle and older sister asked her to do.

Mary's father was a middle-aged man with a thickening waistline, and a crooked but easy smile and gracious manner. His dressed plainly in navy slacks, a striped shirt, and tan, zippered jacket. He didn't speak a word of English – and Mary later told me that his Mandarin also was pretty slim – so we mostly nodded at each other and smiled as Mary translated. In Foshan, as in much of South China, it still is entirely possible to speak only Cantonese, and leave translation with the rest of the world to others.

After saving me from my ridiculous encounter with the motorcycle taxis, we piled into the Toyota, and took off for a traditional Cantonese breakfast at a restaurant on the second floor of a non-descript concrete building. The restaurant was packed with elderly retirees, but Mary's father clearly was a special case – a host led us past a long line of people waiting for tables and seated us immediately. I already was adept at pouring tea methodically over all of my utensils, and rinsing my plates and bowls into a central plastic tub in the middle of the table. With the table now properly set, we went to choose our dishes from huge steam tables and counters, where restaurant staff scurried to keep refilling hundreds of options for small plates and bowls of food. This was a really big and impressive dim sum operation.

Mary led me on a tour through all the options before we chose what we wanted. There were of course a huge selection of steamed buns, dumplings, fried rolls, chicken wings with various flavors, intestines of various types in an array of sauces, and congee with dozens of toppings such as fermented fish, pickled blossoms, and root vegetables. Then, there was the live food section. We took to calling this the "death row" in every good Cantonese restaurant, where patrons walked past cages and pointed to what they wanted to eat. Here, the selection was staggering – there were the usual chickens, ducks, rabbits, geese, tanks of fish and shellfish – but also trays of slugs and cages filled with snakes. A man in the corner squatted on the floor, patiently deboning snakes into long thin fillets. In another area, large glass bottles held dead ferrets, mice, rats, and bugs suspended in alcohol. Mary told me that drinking the liquor was believed to cure ailments. I asked her if she would drink it, and she quickly laughed and replied "Oh no, just old people would do that." Mary's little 'sister' told me that wouldn't eat most of the dim sum options – her favorite food was KFC fried chicken.

After lunch, we began our tour with a walk through China's oldest surviving pottery production center in Shiwan, which is dominated by the famous Nanfeng Kilns, first fired more than five hundred years ago. These enormous and impressive "dragon" kilns were built to climb up the city's several hills. When the fire was lit at the bottom, the heat rose efficiently through adjoining chambers, and Foshan's potters were able to maximize economical production of wares that soon were floated down the Pearl River, out to Hong Kong harbor -- and from there shipped to dining rooms in Boston, Barbados, and London. Foshan, Mary proudly told me, has been the "world's factory" for hundreds of years.

Near the climbing kilns, we passed an ancestral temple of the Wu family. Inside, middle-aged couples were singing Cantonese opera together before a shrine holding tablets honoring their ancestors. They had brought along a picnic, and a boom box connected to microphones, from which they were crooning the high-pitched wailing typical of opera in China. As Mary explained, this was a normal part of Chinese New Year rituals. The temple was a charming example of Lingnan style, with its green ceramic roof tiles flying into extended upturned eaves at the corners, and with sculptural friezes of characters in folk stories on the gable ends and ridge lines. This was not the first or last time that I would stand speechless in the face of a scene so poignant and irreconcilable with my expectations of a grim factory town.

Not far from every disconcerting intrusion of new China, there almost always was an equally charming vestige of its living past.

After our tour of the kilns, and nearby porcelain ceramics showrooms, we headed out of town to the South China Sea Cultural Garden at Xiqiao Mountain – the site of a two hundred foot-tall statue of Kwan-yin, located at Daxian peak. Before beginning our ascent, Mary pulled me over to a small booth, where a matronly woman stood before a huge metal pot over a small burner set on the ground. Mary's father paid her a few yuan, and she served each of us a ladleful of warm, custardy tofu, mixed with sugar and fresh ginger. For such a simple concoction, it was astonishingly delicious, and made me wish that I could replace every dry bag of GORP I ever dutifully consumed with this heavenly mixture. Peering ahead, the massive architectural construction of the shrine and statue, and the beautiful landscaping were dramatic and impressive. An hour later, though, the view from the top was less inspiring; as in Guangzhou, the reward for the long hike was a sprawling view of gray concrete buildings seen through a thick layer of smog.

As we were driving to Mary's home village in another district of the City, her father asked if I wanted to see his factory, and of course I said yes. He turned down a long and empty road to a complex of low buildings and hangars at the end. Workers were on their last day of break from the New Year's vacation, but some were trickling back. As the car pulled up, a security guard opened a gate, and employees scurried to open the car doors and greet Mary's father. She told me that they were "quite nervous" around the boss. I put aside my concerns about living conditions, worker safety, etc., and tried to see the factory through the eyes of the family, who obviously were enormously proud of their new wealth. (I clearly wasn't going to get an unscripted tour anyway.) From the outside, I could see that the factory was made up of its own tight-knit little compound, with dorms and a cafeteria close to the workrooms. All of it was dreary and undecorated, but looked well-maintained and orderly. The substantial security surrounding the factory was less comforting -- a good reminder that orderliness was mandatory and perhaps not always in a friendly way. Guards had to let you in – and out.

Mary's father led me on a tour that obviously was often given to clients. First, we went inside the enormous hangar-like work buildings lined with machines from crude and strong metal shapers and cutters, to lasers doing much finer manufacturing. The noise must have been deafening when all these machines were running, since they mostly were molding metal sheets into casings for lighting fixtures. In the showroom, I got to see examples of the company's products – walls lined with twinkling colored lights, large signs advertising businesses, and pictures of enormous buildings and bridges sporting fantastic light shows in colorful combinations on their sleek surfaces. Light-show displays seem to be on the checklist of every up-and-coming Asian city, and Mary's father obviously had grown prosperous satisfying that huge demand. Finally, we drank tea sitting on comfy leather chairs in a large office – clearly, the space for sealing deals.

After a tour designed to show that Mary's family was definitely on the wealthy side, I was surprised then to continue heading out of town on a quiet road, to a small village of narrow lanes and tall, old, and worn residential buildings clustered tightly together. This was Chen village, and for as long as anyone can remember, it has been the home of the Chens. Because the family has documentation recording that they have lived there for many generations, they possess a particular form of Chinese title (more like an indefinite lease) on the homes. Technically, the Chinese government owns all the land in the country, and long-term leases are the closest anyone can get to property ownership.

We walked down a narrow alley from a small parking lot, and Mary's grandmother and parents, as well as her aunts, uncles and cousins, all came out into the courtyard of one of the houses to greet me. The courtyard was small, but efficiently used, with a raised concrete basin in the front (to hold swimming dinner ingredients until the final moment), fruit trees at center, and towards the back, an angry barking dog that I was warned against approaching.

As usual, everything was made of cement and tile. This was the home of Mary's Aunt and Uncle – her father's brother. Their mother, Grandmother Chen smiled from ear to ear as she greeted me; she appeared to be well into her eighties. Like most elderly Guangdong women, she was small, fit and spry, with deeply wrinkled hands and face, and missing teeth. Smiling with her toothless grin, she plucked a starfruit from the tree just next to her, loaded with fruit, and handed it to me, beaming. She seemed delighted when I devoured it right away. Mary pointed out that the pond and fields behind the house produced most of the food eaten by the family. We waved at her grandfather, on the other side of the pond, picking greens for dinner, and he waved back, and then piloted a small boat towards us. Mary told me that she and her brother and cousins liked to swim in the pond in the hot summer, but it was mostly for raising fish.

Before dinner, I got a tour of the house. The three stories were all exceptionally high – at least twelve feet – in order to draw hot air upwards during Foshan's unbearably hot summers. Ceiling fans cooled the large rooms. Walls that were stained with age and mildew also were covered with children's drawings and prize ribbons from Mary's cousins' athletic events. The floors, made of pale green tile throughout, were soaked with condensation. Although there were definitely signs of "modernity" – chiefly computer technology -- the house otherwise was filled with furniture and objects that had not been changed in decades – including an ancestral shrine on the back wall of the main living area, which held recent offerings of fruit and incense.

During dinner, I wasn't able to participate in what was obviously a very lively conversation. Only Mary, her brother, and cousin spoke Mandarin – the rest of the family spoke only Cantonese. I was racking my brain to listen for any words I understood – after two months of intermittent study, I had made laughably little progress. Through bits and pieces of translation from Mary, however, I did learn something about the history of the Chens.

Grandma and Grandpa Chen did not have much formal education, and had rarely left the village – in fact, they did not like to travel, preferring instead to stay on their homestead where they gardened, raised fish and chickens, and socialized with family members. When it came time for their sons to marry, the Chens traveled to neighboring villages, and arranged betrothals to suitable young women. It was the job of these daughters-in-law to care for them, so the decision was important to everyone. Mary's father and mother seemed to live somewhat separate lives.

Despite the family's wealth, the older Chens clearly maintained ancient customs with fastidious loyalty – but changes small and large also were obvious. After dinner, when I visited Mary's grandmother's house, I noticed that she had a good-sized shrine in the living room that she made offerings to each day . . . the shrine sat next to a television set where she also watched her favorite soap operas.

Changes in the lives of the younger Chen generations, however, were much more profound. I asked Mary if she or any of her friends would be interested in living in Chen village, or having her parents involved in arranging a marriage, and she looked at me as if I was crazy – of course not. It wasn't necessarily expected anymore that a woman would live with her in-laws and care for them in their old age. People in rural areas with little education might do those things, but the children of newly-rich, semi-urban families were not likely to follow this tradition. Good jobs might require moving to a different city, and young people often fell in love with students from distant towns at university.

Chen village hasn't changed much (except for the phone lines and Internet), but the young Chen certainly have. Crammed around a huge round table, the Chen adults and I shared a traditional dinner of chicken, fish, and three kinds of greens cooked in a communal pot of boiling water set on a portable burner, served with rice and a dipping sauce of soy, garlic, and ginger – the same dinner they had eaten every Winter night for as long as anyone could remember. In the meantime, upstairs, Mary's youngest cousins spent their last vacation day arguing about whose turn it was to play games on the computer, and dreaming about the next time they could eat at a KFC.

The insularity of the older members of the Chen family did not surprise me especially, although it was more impressive than other examples I had seen. Our neighborhood at Guangdong University is filled with similar family units, though with far less space to spread out. When we first arrived in our three-bedroom apartment in August, I thought it interesting that two rooms had large beds, and one a smaller bed (which of course made for some horse-trading by the boys). A little while later, it dawned on me that our apartment was not designed for a family with two children. The two large rooms at each end of the small hallway were for the mother and father, and for the father's parents; the small room in between was for the one permitted grandchild.

On any given day or evening, our GDUFS street was filled with those only children – packed onto grandmothers' backs in flimsy cloth carriers, or strapped into strollers pushed by grandfathers. These were the most cocooned and coddled babies I have ever seen, padded in thick quilted suits even when the temperatures were relatively warm, and fanned constantly in the hot summer months. There were no cribs, playpens, or high chairs in sight. On my walk to class each morning, I delighted in watching the informal baby/grandparent social hour held in front of the library at GDUFS. When you add adorable grandparents to an adorable baby, the effect is particularly intoxicating. Under the care of doting retirees, the babies were held almost constantly, and when they began to toddle away, their grandparents were always close behind. If they didn't want to walk, grandparents carried them at any orthopedic cost. My students referred to this next generation of one-child policy grandchildren as "the little emperors and princesses."

Most noticeably absent were the parents. This is the traditional family structure in China; paternal grandparents move in with their son and his wife and raise their grandchild, leaving both father and mother free to work outside the home during their prime years. Retirement in China is technically mandatory for women at 55, and for men at 60, which increases the available nanny-pool (although people have told me of many exceptions to this rule, depending on the province and position). Professors who have been promoted may work longer, but those lower in the rankings generally are forced to comply. The government recently has proposed further laws to support this traditional, family-friendly pattern, including penalties for failure to at least visit parents on a regular basis.

In some ways, this all sounds much more sensible and even wonderful compared to the day care nightmare most working parents face in America, but there also are problems. The transition to urban life is often not so easy for parents imported from rural villages to watch a grandchild while parents pursue professional careers. The biggest sticking points are language and education. China's new generation of professional, urban thirty-somethings were born and raised after the Cultural Revolution – they benefitted from Deng Xiaoping's reform and opening movement, and they learned to speak Mandarin.

Their parents, on the other hand, were raised in an era in which schools were largely shuttered. Many of the elderly transplants in Guangzhou speak only a local hometown dialect, and spend their days isolated from the world around them. Sadly, many are scarred from living through the terrifying purges of their youth, afraid to ever discuss politics, or engage in activities outside their small sphere. Several of my colleagues admitted that their parents are eager to return to their home villages as soon as their grandchild begins school. Their world of "cultural transmit" and "inner spiritual essence" revolved around those places – there could never be another place where they felt at home, or at peace.

After my visit to Foshan, I had a discussion with Mary about study abroad, and she was interested, but clearly did not want to stray from Chen village for too long. She and her father and mother lived in an apartment in the new part of the city, but this village was their touchstone – the place they clearly belonged – and they were tied to this land by the weight of ancestral bonds stretching back hundreds of years in an unbroken chain – there was no way to know exactly how far back, given that most records were destroyed during the Cultural Revolution.

Very few Americans have a Chen village – our

ancestors typically come from different regions of the world, and most of us consider education and employment opportunities more important than staying on the same street as our parents. I know few people who do anything akin to visiting the graves of their ancestors in America, or singing opera to them on Memorial Day. Alienation from ancestral roots feels natural for families like mine who chose to come to America, but for slaves like Frederick Douglass, it was a searing wound.

My student who wrote that the removal of a slave child from the family "is more serious than the segregation or even the genocide because it avoids the cultural links, the inner spiritual essence, be instilled into the new generation" understood Douglass' words in a light that was new to me. Another agreed: "I think the slaveholder in the text tried to avoid communication between mother and her little son because he did not want the little boy to know too much about himself and the little boy could be easier to be controlled in that way." Many of my students wrote with a similar assumption: that a person couldn't be whole without the identity that comes from family and place. These students understood that Frederick Douglass and millions of other American slaves never had the opportunity to come from a place like Chen village, and empathized with that loss much more keenly than I ever could.

Chapter Two. Progress: The American Centennial and the Chinese Century

In November 2011, my friend and fellow-Fulbrighter Ann Bartow travelled to visit one of her students in a small village outside Shanghai. She later told me that after a night on a rock-hard bed, she woke up to a frigid morning in her student's unheated family home, and had to break through the ice in her water glass to brush her teeth. Based on her report, and knowing nothing about Mary's family situation, I journeyed to Foshan prepared with extra socks and gloves, and bottled water. As it turned out, I should have brought my bathing suit and a split of champagne.

After dinner, Mary's father drove us back to the massive, sterile new park in downtown Foshan, where we watched young lovers send messages regarding their hopes for the future into the thick night air inside red paper lanterns, each holding a small candle as propulsion. The Lantern Festival was the last event that welcomed the New Year, and thousands had come out to watch and participate in this venerable ancient tradition, albeit in a thoroughly re-made environment. As I looked around, the expectation of bright futures for these young Chinese lovers was palpable. Certainly, Mary and her cousins have a range of educational and career opportunities that were unimaginable to their parents in their own youth, growing up as they had in the darkest throes of brutal poverty and repression in China in the 1960s and 1970s.

After a while, we walked over to the Intercontinental Hotel, where Mary's father had booked us all rooms – mine was on the club floor (!), with a view looking directly out over the man-made lake. This was the ultimate in *guanxi* – a gift intended to cement my friendship with the Chen family. I was deeply embarrassed that I had brought only Vermont maple candies and a set of decorative chopsticks as my own form of *guanxi* -- but what could I say except "thank you"? All of Mr. Chen's business clients stayed there, and to turn down the gift would have been extremely rude. Plus, I really wanted to take a long soak in the bathtub – and sleep in a soft bed with a ridiculous number of pillows.

Late that night, standing in a thick bathrobe and looking out my enormous picture window at the lights of the new city below, I could see a platoon of earthmovers and cranes standing by, ready to plow on towards the finished result of the new Foshan – the completion of yet another spectacular example of why this has been called "China's Century." As an historian of America's gilded age and progressive era, it was hard not to be overwhelmed by the feeling of *déjà vu* – America had been there, and done that.

In May, 1876, President Ulysses S. Grant officially opened America's first World's Fair – technically called the "International Exhibition of Arts, Manufactures and Products of the Soil and Mine" – but known by its more informal name as the "Centennial Exposition." Nearing both the end of the Reconstruction Era and the hundredth anniversary of the Declaration of Independence, Americans (especially white Northerners) were ready to put the Civil War behind them, and move ahead with a new confidence born of booming wealth and an impressive record of technological innovations.

The Centennial Exposition covered four hundred and fifty acres of parkland in Philadelphia and featured more than thirty thousand exhibits, including contributions from nearly every country in the world. But the star of the show was clearly America itself – this was our coming-out party – and all the attention was focused on marvels such as Alexander Graham Bell's telephone, Christopher B. Sholes's Remington typewriter, and George Corliss' steam engine. At 70 feet in height and weighing a massive 650 tons, the Corliss Engine was able to power all of the displays in Machinery Hall, including its cutting-edge electric lights and elevators. American manufacturing and economic success were the envy of the world. The homework I assigned for class on this unit included an early review of the show from the *Times* of London: "The American invents as the Greek sculpted and the Italian painted: it is Genius."

At the end of our class on the Reconstruction Era, I presented this next topic by asking students working in groups to make a ranked list of accomplishments that would demonstrate a new nation's great success in the world. My expectation was that they would choose China's incredible building projects – the skyscrapers, dams, railroads, bridges, tunnels, towers, universities, highways, and parks, that routinely earn superlatives such as "largest," "fastest," and "longest" in the world. In short, I thought Chinese students would be most impressed (as I was) by the things I could see from the club floor of the Intercontinental Hotel in Foshan.

Given my expectations, their number one pick – "famous Professors" -- truly surprised me, to the point that I actually gasped out loud. Following close behind were "important scientists" and "excellent artists" – in short, the kind of inventive genius they idolized in Americans from Alexander Graham Bell to Steve Jobs. One student wrote in his homework: "The increase of the number of patents granted by the federal patent office manifests that the united states, the young and exuberant country, was becoming highly innovative. . . Nevertheless, it was only a starting point from which numerous innovative inventions were to flourish in the upcoming years to shape America into the world's superpower." It was intelligence, creativity, and innovation – not sheer force of construction – that most impressed my students.

As I was to discover, my students, and many others that I spoke to in China, were deeply ambivalent about the same aspects of China's growth that Americans today tend to view as spectacular. Students told me privately that the buildings that amaze me were constructed on land confiscated from poor farmers who had no say in the matter, often with little or no compensation. And they said that construction was often shoddy and dangerous, thanks to contracts that were awarded to builders who simply gave the biggest kickbacks to rich and well connected Party members. The students clearly saw their country through a different lens than I had assumed. This became especially apparent on the several occasions when Chinese colleagues and students asked me directly: "Do you think China is a developing nation?" It was always an awkward question, but they seemed to really want an outside take, as though they couldn't figure out the answer on their own.

During our first months in Guangzhou, Graham, Emmett and I frequently returned to a conversation about what it meant to call China a "developing nation." Our frame of reference was definitely skewed. We were living in one of the richest cities, in the richest province of China. Also, we were living on the campus of a reasonably well-funded and beautifully landscaped university, in an apartment building with new furniture and modern appliances. When we travelled to wealthier parts of the city, we saw tall apartment buildings, sleek and impressive business complexes, and crowds of shoppers and beautifully dressed professionals filling sparkling new malls.

On the other hand, people did live in very crowded

conditions, even in this wealthy city, and there frequently were smells that reminded us that public amenities such as drinking water and waste removal were not up to generally-accepted U.S. standards. It was pretty clear from the dripping pipes and fetid smell in our concrete neighborhood that more than water was flowing downstream into the stream that ran through campus. Nobody we knew in China drank the tap water without boiling it, the air quality was a disaster, and garbage littered the streets outside of wealthy business areas in downtown Guangzhou. And while there weren't a large number of panhandlers, those we saw were extremely disturbing, with severe bodily injuries and disabilities.

Still, I thought that the answer was pretty clear – I didn't see how anyone could call China a developing nation now, especially given the extraordinary progress the country has made in the last thirty years at boosting literacy rates, and reducing poverty. Somalia is a developing nation, not China. It wasn't until April that I rethought my position, and understood the indecision of my Chinese friends: Guangzhou definitely was not the whole story of the "real" China.

One of the best parts of the Fulbright lecture program was the opportunity to travel throughout China on speaking tours. At the start of each year, the State Department circulates a list of visiting scholars and their lecture topics, and urges universities around the country to invite scholars in to speak. Although I definitely took full advantage of this opportunity over the course of ten different three-day trips, I only spoke to audiences at fairly large universities in big cities that all were definitely "developed." In April, however, Fred and I took the opportunity to travel as tourists in a rural area of Yunnan Province with our friends Keith and Ann. Keith is a dear compatriot from Vermont, with whom we had served many years on our local school board, and Ann already was a frequent travel buddy, on break from teaching intellectual property law courses at Tonji University in Shanghai. They both were cheerful, patient travel companions during a wonderful but exhausting 10-day trip that took us, at least in part, to a more "real" China.

Our visit to Yunnan began with a two-hour plane flight west and north to Kunming, the capital of the Province, and then a shorter leg further north to the touristy city of Dali, nestled between the Cangshan mountain range and beautiful Lake Erhai. Here, the air was clear, and the skies blue. Our inn was located just outside the tall city walls of Dali's ancient Ming-Dynasty downtown. Once we passed through the high-arching gate, we entered a largely preserved (or at least well-recreated) ancient town, with stone roadways and colorfully decorated houses with tile roofs.

Yunnan province is famous for many things – Pu'er tea, tobacco, coffee bean cultivation, and beautiful mountainous scenery. But perhaps mostly, it is known for its rich ethnic diversity. On a leisurely bike ride outside the walls of the city, we passed verdant fields of rice and beans, tended by women and men in colorful outfits signifying their various ethnic affiliations. The areas we visited were populated chiefly by Bai and Yi people -- recognizable by their distinctive blue batik smocks and elaborate headdresses -- and also Naxi people, who are famous for their matriarchal and female-dominant social order. One of our Naxi drivers had his daughter along for the day because, as he told us, his wife had run away with another man – a "typical Naxi woman," he complained. Ann and I joked about concocting a "Feminist Trail" for tourists to match the famous "Hippie Trail," and putting Naxi land on the map.

In addition to our visits to the typical tourist destinations of Dali and Lijiang, which were lovely, we also took time as well to explore a far less trodden path in the region. In the course of my web searches to plan our vacation, I came across the description of an ancient temple / theater that had been renovated into a small inn outside the village of Shaxi, north and slightly west of Dali. Shaxi is the best-preserved town on the "tea and horse caravan trail" that brought those important commodities, as well as salt, from Tibet through the mountains to China, beginning in the Tang Dynasty more than a thousand years ago.

For a reasonable fee, the inn arranged transportation from Dali to the inn in a mini-van, and then for another very modest fee, arranged for an overnight homestay in a tiny Bai village called Ma Ping Guan, which is hundreds of years old, and accessible only on foot or by donkey. Everyone trusted me to make the arrangements, and so I went ahead and booked the trip for the middle of our adventure, without much more information than that.

The ride from Dali to Shaxi provided our typical awe regarding the pace of change in China. During nearly all of our drive, a massive, half-finished highway under construction weaved in and out near the narrow, worn road on which we were traveling. When the new highway is finished, it will bring tourists and commodities from Kunming all the way to "Shangri-La" – a distance of more than four hundred miles through steep mountainous slopes. And above the highway, many of the ridgelines in our eyesight were topped by massive wind turbines, spinning slowly and elegantly in the mountain breezes, delivering electricity to the villages in the basins below.

Shaxi itself had none of these awe-inspiring visions of "progress." Instead, the van dropped us at the center of a fertile basin, surrounded by fields of mostly rice and beans. At regular intervals, all along the edges of the basin, small villages dotted the landscape, each with narrow winding

streets that snaked between ancient courtyard houses. Each
village had its own ancestral temple, and in charming
fashion, a theater for performing opera to please both local
deities and familial spirits. In the mornings, adult villagers
led basket- and tool-laden donkeys out to the fields, where
they spent hours hunched over rice shoots, pulling weeds
from swampy marshes. At sunset, they trod back home,
where grandparents presumably were preparing dinner.
There was a pretty even mix of trucks and horses or donkeys
on the paved roads. At frequent intervals, these roads served
an extra purpose beyond getting from one place to another;
farmers laid dried stalks of rice or beans out, so that both
kinds of beasts – motor and animal – could do their threshing
for them.

After a first relaxing evening at the inn, we joined our
guide -- a local schoolteacher – at mid-morning the next day
for the hike to Ma Ping Guan, where we would stay with his
parents in a traditional Bai courtyard home. The trail was
dusty, and as we climbed higher and higher into the
mountains, we passed trailside stone and cement tombs, and
a small shrine near spring-fed water. The steep and narrow
path was littered with donkey scat, and occasionally by
garbage left behind by villagers, for whom this was the only
road to town. Despite the enchanting scenes of the rice fields
and clay-tiled village roofs of Shaxi valley seen from high
above, we were absolutely exhausted when we arrived. Our
climb had been four hours long, on a bright, dry day without
enough water, and essentially straight up. We had gained
almost three thousand feet, and now were perched just under
ten thousand feet in altitude. When we finally looked down
into tiny Ma Ping Guan, we saw a cluster of ancient buildings
in various states of decay, and a beautiful covered bridge,
with decorative woodcarvings leaping out from its eaves.
Our guide on the hiking path spoke very little English but he

stayed with us long enough to take us on a tour of the various structures in the village, before he raced back down the path to his job and home.

Our first stop was the house where we would be staying. It was a bit shocking. One room had a mud floor, and one of the two beds was made of a large sack stuffed with straw. The second bedroom had been fixed up with some linoleum flooring, and a television. Unfortunately, in the middle of the night we discovered that the room was also used for food storage, and so Ann and I lay awake throughout much of the night listening to the terrifying scratching and screeching of gluttonous rats. Our hosts, whose names I could not pronounce, were probably in their early sixties, but they looked much older than that. Both wore the distinctive blue cloth made and worn by Bai people, with Communist Mao caps, and high necklines. Neither of them had many teeth. The wife spent a while in the kitchen, stoking an open fire that heated some dishes she soon brought out. Her husband had set out a small child-size table, with stools around it. We ate beans, pickled vegetables, and preserved pork fat, while the family's horse, dog, and chickens roamed freely in the courtyard. Our host repeatedly offered us puffs from a water pipe made from a stub of PVC pipe, in which he had stuffed both fresh tobacco leaves, and rolled cigarettes. As politely as possible, we indicated that we didn't smoke.

After our meal, their son took us for the rest of our tour. He showed us the village temple and theater, and proudly told us that villagers still return at the New Year, to perform opera for the Gods, and take care of ancestral tombs. A long list of people who had given money to keep the temple standing was nailed to one of the walls. Unfortunately, many of the painted decorations in the temple had been actively scrubbed away, the angry residue of that violent act left painfully exposed. I saw these destructive vestiges of the Cultural Revolution all over China. Another ancient building in Ma Ping Guan – a pagoda, had been converted into a Party propaganda center, with loudspeakers attached to the eaves for delivering "news." Upstairs, a small shrine still held its god. Someone had recently brought up some flowers and incense. I rarely saw a temple or shrine in China that wasn't actively tended.

Finally, our tour guide brought us to the village store, which sold staples like oil, soy sauce, beer, soda, cigarettes, baijou (a grim alcoholic beverage derived from rice), and phone cards for adding value to cellular plans. The provincial government had gone to great expense to string electrical wires all the way up to Ma Ping Guan, and a cellular tower loomed above us. The wires continued along a narrow path even further up into the mountains, and our guide said that if you walked for two more hours you came to a Yi village – another stop on the route to Tibet.

We bought some beer and baijou, and headed back towards the house. There was just one more site to see – the abandoned school, which still had a cement trench we could use as a toilet (our hosts used the same shed as the horse). There was a broom conveniently laid by the trench to whisk away flies. Years before, the school had been closed, and the children sent to Shaxi to live and study. Now, the village felt abandoned, with fewer than three hundred residents left. Most of them were elderly people, with just a few younger people looking after them. Garbage was strewn throughout the town, including an enormous number of empty baijou bottles. It seemed as though people had given up on taking care of Ma Ping Guan, as though it was a remnant of the past, without a future.

Sitting on the steps of the courtyard the next morning, groggy from extreme discomfort and lack of sleep, I saw an adorable preschool-aged girl in a pink tracksuit peek her head out from the house across the way, clearly curious. When I waved, she burst into tears and ran back in the house. Her grandmother came out and stared at me, then went inside. I didn't get the sense that many other tourists had found this website. And I'm not sure everyone in our party was happy I had.

Whether or not my friends will ever sign up for my tour-planning services again, I was glad we went to Ma Ping Guan, because it gave me a visceral understanding of why my students had a hard time answering the question of whether China is still a developing country. They didn't question that designation because of places like Guangzhou, but rather because of the condition of life in rural villages like Ma Ping Guan, where some had been raised, and where many still returned to visit elderly relatives.

But there was another more complicated reason as well. Our Bai hosts, like the vast majority of Chinese, have no say over whether the village school will be repaired, or whether the government might decide to "restore" a place like Ma Ping Guan as a "Disney-fied" tourist destination, as seems possible given the investment in the massive highway, electrical lines, wind turbines, and cell tower. A student wrote to me by e-mail, enraged when we discussed some aspects of American politics that triggered her anger about her own situation at home:

> in my village, many of us don't know who our "local governor" is and these local officials made deal with real estate agency without announcement to villagers. It irritated all of us that our former local governor sold most of our land, the public property at a very very cheap price and most of our villagers didn't know about it untill they got a meagre share of the "profits" from selling land. This happend about ten years ago when most of us didn't get the sufficient

ideas about legal rights. Recent years more and more news reported about similar situations and woke up the legal awareness among the public so nowadays the public knows how to fight for their rights. Nevertheless, there are still many so-called officials took advantage of local residents.

Stories like this made me realize that attitudes towards the concepts of "development" and "progress" are shaped not only by fears about what is lost, but perhaps even more by the process by which decisions about change are made. Who gets to decide? And who profits? Considering those questions made the roots of my students' ambivalence much more apparent. "Progress" is much less appealing if you are on the losing side of the deal.

When I first arrived in China, I adopted the rookie-diplomat habit of complimenting my host country excessively. I emphasized how much Americans are fascinated by China's rise and power, and the amazing speed at which it has transformed. I even waxed (only half-heartedly) about the benefits of central planning as compared with our own country, and used the stories of two roads to explain a dimension of democracy that is sometimes disadvantageous. Criticizing my own country was always the best way to initiate a much more honest discussion about China. Here's the story I liked to tell:

Back in Vermont, I live not far from a stretch of roadway known as the Southern Connector. It was planned more than twenty years ago to take traffic from our major highway – I89 – and move it efficiently to the downtown without disturbing Burlington's southern residential neighborhoods. Half of it was built, and then construction stopped when money and legal troubles began. There's a Superfund site in the way, and the project requires local, state, and federal cooperation, which has not been forthcoming. Throughout my seventeen years in Burlington, the Southern Connector has been in the news on and off almost constantly, including crowded and angry community meetings, interested parties' briefs, government agency reports and studies, and nasty letters to the editor of our local newspaper on both sides. Despite all of that effort and energy, the Connector is still a half-built, half-deteriorated concrete road, going nowhere, supporting lots of weeds and occasional skateboarding kids. And tractor-trailer trucks still rumble down quiet residential streets on their way into Burlington, causing danger, noise, and annoyance.

In contrast, I witnessed a road built at Baiyunshan (Baiyun Mountain), the park next door to our apartment, in less than a month. The name translates as White Cloud Mountain, and the area has been prized for its natural beauty since as far back as the Warring States Period, twenty-five hundred years ago. The ridgeline at Baiyun includes more than thirty peaks, many topped by pagodas or cell towers, and there also are a variety of attractions, including an aviary, cable car rides, waterfalls, steep hikes, and a posh resort and conference center. We were incredibly lucky to live next to this gorgeous park, but in typical clueless fashion I had no idea it was even there during my first week in Guangzhou.

I only became aware of the park because of my curiosity about a cacophony that began outside my bedroom window every morning at 5:30 a.m. It sounded like people were singing, playing traditional Chinese songs on scratchy portable tape players, clapping, and shouting, all about fifteen feet from my window, on the other side of a high wall that blocked my vision. One morning, I got dressed and found the end of the wall so I could get on the other side. And there they were – crowds of Chinese retirees, moving in a steady stream from a main road and parking area to a park entrance, down a narrow street.

Nearest my apartment, the street was littered with piles of garbage – mostly bottles, wrappers, and plastic bags. Farther up, vendors perched on either side of the road, their wares spread out on burlap sacks, or sheets of cardboard. There were fruits and vegetables, sundries like nail clippers and knives, exercise clothes, root vegetables, dried herbs used as medicines, live frogs, eels, snakes, rabbits, and chickens (to be killed and cleaned after the customers selected them). There was another vendor who sold fish and crocodiles -- thankfully already dead. Finally, I found the gate to Baiyunshan. Once I paid my five RMB (about eighty cents), I was in a completely different world.

On the other side of the gate, a dirt road led through a grove of enormous and graceful bamboo clumps, which made a delightful clicking sound when the wind stirred. Here, there was no garbage, or vendors with their screeching chickens. Many of the elderly neighbors who came to the park brought bottles to collect water from springs and streams and carry it home in heavy backpacks, or on rickety luggage carriers. In a large reservoir not far from the entrance, some people used plastic bottles as flotation devices, and added a morning swim to their walk. Victorious told me not to swim in the water. I'm not sure if he thought it was polluted, or just dangerous to swim in general, but in either case I followed his advice. Nevertheless, I tried to walk in Baiyunshan at least a few days a week.

Mostly, my walks were uneventful. I passed the vendors, strolled for an hour, and then bought some groceries for the day on the road back to the apartment. But one day, in early October, I noticed bulldozers alongside the dirt path inside the park gate, ripping out huge swaths of bamboo clumps. By the next week, a new asphalt road had been paved. A week later, a team of landscapers wearing straw hats arrived with trucks full of lush green plants. Within a few days, they had planted a gorgeous and abundant selection of semi-tropical shrubs and flowers – and even replanted some bamboo. In week three, construction teams built a new bathroom, two brick paths through the bamboo forest, and a couple of attractive bridges, looking out over newly-constructed waterfalls. Did this damage the bird, fish, and frog population? Probably. Did anyone stop to hold a public meeting? Definitely not. Central planners made the plans, and poof, now it was done.

I diplomatically told the story of these two roads to illustrate my respect and admiration for China's amazing progress to my new colleagues and students. But they never took the bait. Instead, my little parable elicited raised eyebrows, cynical rebuttals, snorts, and eye rolling. After that, I stopped complimenting the benefits of central planning.

China's "progress" in the eyes of the world is based on the things that impressed me in Foshan, and in Baiyunshan -- financial growth, production capacity, and massive, swiftly-executed infrastructure projects. But my new Chinese friends clearly didn't see progress through the same lens. This made for an especially interesting conversation about America's Gilded Age.

On an exam for my American Culture seminar, I posed the following question: "Studying the history and culture of another country often provides new insight and understanding to your own country as well. Discuss three examples of materials from our course that may be compared and/or contrasted with Chinese experience in interesting ways." Not surprisingly, many students chose to write about the Centennial Exposition. Their attitudes towards China's equivalent "progress" varied widely. On the optimistic side, one student wrote:

In 1876, America presented itself as an emerging

power through the magnificent Centennial Exhibition in Philadelphia. The event marked the rise of American national identity characterized by pride, confidence, and exuberance. In 2008, China shared the similar experience: the Beijing Olympic games. Like Americans, Chinese felt an unprecedentedly strong sense of national identity and pride as they saw their edge-cutting technology, glorious culture and enormous prospect. Yet before the games, China was shadowed by the Tibetan riot and Wenchan earthquakes. Pain, fury, and grief pervaded the land in the face of past trauma and future hope, Chinese looked forward as Americans did.

Another student compared the two nations' experiences with a less positive spin:

After the Civil War, America developed rapidly and raised in the world as a young and powerful nation. Through the exhibition at Centennial and comments from astonished Europeans, we caught a glimpse of American's proud and confidence in itself. On the contrary, China at that time was suffering from the exploitation of capitalist countries. But before the opening of its door to the world, China used to be very innocently proud. This proud, however, is different from America's in the end of the 19th Century. China had been almost complete separated from the world, thus she was so arrogant of her own possessions. As for America, though it might be accused of over confident, its material affluence could be implicitly seen. Besides, China's pride led to her fast decay while America's gave its people optimism for future development.

For this young graduate student, pride was not necessarily a deserved Chinese attribute, nor a healthy attitude for the country. Our nation, celebrating its independence from colonial authority, had a lot to celebrate compared to a nation intermittently threatened and occupied for hundreds of years. A third student considered the weight of China's history as a detriment:

> America and China are profoundly distinct from each other in terms of its history and tradition. America is a young country with amazing exuberance. Instead of "looking into the past," American prefers to "look forward." In the 1876 Centennial Exposition, new inventions and technology were highlighted to show its creativity and great potential in the future. In contrast, China is an old country with thousand years of history. There is no doubt that China benefits a lot from its past. However, too much nostalgia of glorious past will hinder the development of this ancient country. It's a tricky question as how to make a balance between its past and future.

Anyone who spends time in China these days is immediately confronted by this "tricky question."

In addition to a lack of community discussion regarding what buildings are built, where the money goes, how parks or altered, or which neighborhoods will get upgraded streets, there also is very little open discussion of what constitutes the Chinese "past" that is worthy of preservation in the face of a dizzying onslaught of "progress."

In an earlier class that semester, I diverged on a bit of a tangent about American perceptions of "good, old days" that – from a historian's perspective – were usually almost entirely erroneous. I asked my students what they thought were China's "good, old days." They had a tough time with that. At first they said the Tang Dynasty, because China was "strong, and not invaded by outsiders." But the next week they came back and said they had been discussing the question outside of class and changed their minds – the good old days were "before there were any Emperors, and the people were empowered." That was a really long time, and many phases of history ago. The traces of that time were impossible to see, or preserve. What has survived in China is almost entirely a landscape fraught with bad old times.

When Fred and I visited Ann in Shanghai, we brought along our Lonely Planet guide – then a few years old – and used the map inside to try and find what was described as the heart of the French Concession. After circling a huge construction zone for half an hour, puzzling at our guide, and the street signs, we finally realized that the pit was what we were looking for. This historic area of stately homes and government buildings built by the Colonial winners of the dreadful Opium Wars simply had been bulldozed away. Our two-year old guidebook was irrelevant.

Americans grappled with a different sense of historical dislocation in their own Century, as the Centennial ushered in an unprecedented wave of Colonial Revival style – in everything from furniture, to architecture, to literature. In China, individuals don't get to decide what style to build in that might make them feel safer or more at peace with "progress" – whether that might be the Tang Dynasty or something else.

The people I met in China are sometimes optimistic, but more often they are deeply cynical about the changes that take place around them so swiftly, and without any opportunity for public comment. I used to make a joke about the trajectory of my years spent on our local school board – that I had started out so excited to hear what everyone thought of our plans at public comment sessions, but after six years grew to see it as an annoying waste of time. After living in China, I will never see public comment as a waste of time again . . . and I may even take a stroll over to the Southern Connector just to bask in its evocation of democracy's grand dysfunction.

Chapter Three. Westward Ho: Native Americans and China's Ethnic Minorities

Fred finally arrived in November, and I arranged for us to spend three days in Hong Kong on our own, giving him some time to adjust before diving into our cramped apartment in Guangzhou with the boys. Hong Kong was a fantastic place for a reunion; there's a reason that so many great films have been made here. Dramatic, lush, mountainous islands rise from one of the world's busiest harbors, forming the backdrop for delicious food, and dazzling colonial and modern architecture. Over the course of frequent trips during the year, I truly fell in love with this ultra-international city.

One of the many reasons I looked forward to our trips to Hong Kong was that I didn't have to work so hard to be understood. As a colony of England for more than a century, the British imprint was discernible everywhere. Plenty of people understood English, and English-language signs and newspapers were ubiquitous. Although the language situation there was easier for me, however, it is a serious problem for Hong Kong residents, chafing under advancing expectations that they will be absorbed linguistically, as well as politically, into Mainland China.

When we first were told that we would be headed to Guangzhou, a friend who is an Asian Studies Professor said "that's too bad for Graham." Unbeknownst to me, the "Chinese" studied in every American (and Chinese) high school is Mandarin, while in South China, most people speak Cantonese. In my own experience, trying to learn the four tones of Mandarin was brutal enough . . . Cantonese has nine. Apparently, foreigners almost never even attempt to learn it.

When I traveled to Hong Kong with the boys, they frequently scolded me for using the few Mandarin phrases I had managed to learn. When I thanked bus drivers and doormen by saying *"xie xie"* they would snarl: "Mom, stop! They don't speak Mandarin here!" In Hong Kong, language is a volatile political issue, inciting prejudice and hostility in both directions. While we were in the city, we saw anti-Mainland posters referring to Chinese as swarms of locusts. As the boys frequently reminded me, speaking Mandarin (albeit badly and accidentally) was considered offensive.

Mandarin instruction has been a major part of efforts to "unify" China for nearly a century, since Nationalist reformers attempted to bind the country together using education as a principle tool. There is a lively academic debate regarding why Mandarin was chosen by Nationalists as the unifying language (some say it lost by one vote to Cantonese), and an even livelier debate about the merits of the official shift from traditional to simplified characters since the 1950s. Sixty years ago, the shift was designed to raise literacy rates; today, an argument for the less authentic simplified characters is that they are easier to integrate with computer software.

China's complicated relationships with Hong Kong, Macau, and Taiwan all are made more complicated by the varying choices each has made regarding what is the "right" Chinese to teach, speak, and write. In Hong Kong and Macau, Cantonese is still the dominant language, and in Taiwan, children are taught the more complicated traditional system of characters. On the Mainland, these arguments are contrastingly purely academic – Mandarin is the only Chinese dialect taught in schools, and almost everyone takes for granted that it is the "official" language they must speak to succeed. Most of my South Chinese students spoke Cantonese to their parents, as well as a third, more remote dialect with their grandparents. Nonetheless, all their education (outside the GDUFS English Department) was offered in Mandarin.

Although Beijing leaders promised "one country, two systems" when Britain ceded its territorial claims and Hong Kong became a Special Administrative Region of China fifteen years ago, recent policy shifts have cast doubt on that promise, such as attempts to impose Mainland "patriotic education" in public schools. In my seminar, when we studied America's own experience of expansion and cultural loss, it was hard not to see an enormous number of similarities. American politicians wrote hundreds of treaties with our own ethnic minorities in the 19th-century, promising something like "two systems" and shared prosperity. Most of those promises were broken; the example was sobering.

In 1876, the Centennial Exposition documented not only America's growing self-confidence on the world stage, but also a great deal of the hostility and discrimination that was pervasive during that era. In class with my students, we spent some time discussing the small and segregated "Women's Pavillion" at the Exposition, which purposefully excluded all references to the growing suffrage movement. In response, Susan B. Anthony led a demonstration at Independence Hall on July 4th, 1876, at which she read a sarcastic and aspirational "Women's Declaration of Independence:"

> . . . We ask of our rulers, at this hour, no special favors, no special privileges, no special legislation. We ask justice, we ask equality, we ask that all the civil and political rights that belong to citizens of the United States, be guaranteed to us and our daughters forever.

My students thought that Anthony should have been free to make her case at the Exposition; women in China face a variety of discriminations, but most of them stem from cultural expectations, not government-sanctioned disenfranchisement.

Discussing treatment of Native Americans at the Exposition was more interesting, because the parallel with China's controversial current events is much more striking. At the Philadelphia Centennial, Native-Americans were exhibited in an "immense array of Indian 'curiosities'" designed to document them before they were completely eradicated by European settlers. As part of the Native American display at the Exposition, life-size manikins and artifacts demonstrated the traditional ways of life of fifty-three tribes. As respectful as this might have seemed, at the same time that East-coast audiences marveled at buckskins, teepees, and baskets, Federal troops in the west were launching large-scale military campaigns against many of these same tribes. In fact, at the height of the Exposition, General George Armstrong Custer was defeated and killed by an army of Sioux warriors at the Battle of the Little Bighorn. This was Native America's last significant victory, and as a result, European-American ire was inflamed, and anti-Indian sentiment intensified. After Little Bighorn, Federal troops savagely implemented land seizures, forced relocations, and suppression of the same traditional cultural attributes celebrated at the Exposition. Many Indian children, removed from their families to boarding schools, were forbidden to speak their native languages and practice their religions.

Anyone who regularly reads Western news coverage of China today is keenly aware that many of these same tragic government activities are well underway. Even within China, reports of uprisings protesting land seizures and repressive cultural policies are not hard to find. During our year in Guangzhou, the *China Daily News* reported numerous suicides by Tibetan Buddhists protesting Chinese rule, as well as a series of riots by ethnic minorities in central and western provinces. Those involved were typically described in the official accounts as "terrorists," "agitators," or even "mentally-ill," but nonetheless it was not practical to control the story of the turbulent protests against repression altogether.

To convey our Native American version of this conflict, I first assigned students to read the Native American chapter of the *Norton Anthology of American Literature*, which includes translations of the Navajo Night Chant, and a number of plaintive songs sung by Ojibwe people in the area of North Dakota and Minnesota. I was able to download modern versions of these on iTunes and play them from my computer, which made for a particularly surreal moment of global technological fusion in our Guangzhou classroom.

Since many of the students were literature majors, they seemed especially to enjoy the lyrical and hypnotic qualities of the Navajo Night Chant, which expresses a petition to the Sacred Mountains and other spirits for healing and good fortune:

... With beauty all around me may I walk.
In old age wandering on a trail of beauty, lively, may I walk.
In old age wandering on a trail of beauty, living again, may I walk.
It is finished in beauty.
It is finished in beauty...

And in light of the history we had been studying, they also were moved by a song that expressed the sadness of the Chippewa people at watching the aftermath of successful battles against their Sioux enemies:

The Sioux women

Pass to and fro wailing
As they gather up
Their wounded men
The voice of their weeping comes back to us

These examples of heartfelt human prayer and empathetic suffering stood in stark contrast to both the stereotypical manikins and harsh caricatures circulating at the Centennial Exposition.

For some students, it was easy to grasp that the Native American story was different than the accounts told by European-Americans. One student wrote:

> The song, *The Sioux Women Gather Up Their Wounded*, which depicts the woeful scene of women collecting their wounded combatants, reveals that even to their enemies, the Chippewa show profound sympathy for their loss. This indicates that Indians, who are stereotyped as barbarian, cruel and uncivilized killers, are actually kind-hearted, compassionate and friendly people. Demeaning Indians is obviously part of the scheme of invasion and conquest.

And another student wrote:

> Under the ideology of Manifest Destiny which was a product of nationalism, white American people assumed the westward expansion would bring more civilized ideas to those indigenous people and thus made their life better. But I personally see from the Chippewa songs a civilized and romantic spirit which makes me think that maybe those American Indian would live a happier life if there had never been any foreign incursions.

One would be hard-pressed to find an American historian who didn't believe that Native Americans would have "lived a happier life" without "white American people."

Although most of my students were clearly empathetic to the beautiful examples of Native culture in the *Norton Anthology*, most also were unwilling to move beyond a dualistic division of Nature (Native) and Culture (European) that basically mirrored the attitudes of most 19th Century Americans, and the majority Han narrative of China's own historical development. One student wrote of the Navajo Night Chant:

> I think there are two aspects that lead to the worship of nature among the Navajos. For one thing, the Navajo tribe, I assume, is still largely uncivilized. If we consider the whole human history as a process of progressing from nature to culture, the Navajos have forwarded but a few steps. Therefore, they are somehow closer and more exposed to nature. . . For another, I think this has something to do with their historical background. When the US takes over their territory, the Navajos, as a relatively backward tribe, supposedly will identify the US army as human civilization or culture. This culture has done great harm to their lives, including destroying their food, driving them to leave their home and even imprisoning them. So, culture to them is rather dark and monstrous, whereas nature is the only place that they can find salvation and refuge. Therefore, they believe that the most sacred spirit lies in nature.

It was easier to get the students to empathize, than to see both communities as equally "civilized" and deserving of a self-defined future. While they might readily admit that their own ethnic minorities would be "happier" without "foreign incursions," they clearly also believed that their future wasn't going to be up to them to decide. Ultimately, most of my students seemed to accept this general assumption, which was quite similar to the position of Americans at the

Centennial Exposition in 1876; they both admired ethnic minority culture . . . and saw it as backwards and therefore doomed in the face of the "progress" of civilization.

Just as I had largely given up on expanding my students' assumptions about the inevitable demise of ethnic minorities, I fortunately had a bit of Internet luck. The night before my last class on Native Americans, I went hunting for a downloadable online video of contemporary Indian life that would demonstrate just how wrong the prognosticators of doom had been. We do, after all, include within our borders hundreds of state- and federally-recognized sovereign Indian nations based on reservations located in thirty-five out of fifty states. They aren't all faring equally well, but nonetheless, I thought this might stimulate some interesting thinking about future possibilities from a different perspective.

After hours of fruitless searching, I finally found a Twin Cities Public Television documentary called "First Speakers," which describes a project to save the Ojibwe language from extinction. The documentary follows the work of Professor Anton Treuer and a team of volunteers, who are recording elders in conversation, creating a dictionary of the language, and teaching Ojibwe and English equally, at two experimental dual-language elementary schools on Minnesota reservations.

Towards the end of class, I showed a ten-minute segment of the documentary and asked the students (playing devil's advocate) whether they thought the effort was a waste of time. After all, if the children were educated to speak Ojibwe -- a language known by less than one thousand people, how would that help them get into college, or get a job? This was a language (as a skeptic in the video pointed out) that had "no economic value." Without realizing it, I had hit a nerve that ran deep.

Some of the students became emotional – it was clear that they were conflicted. They weren't thinking about Ojibwe, or even Cantonese, but rather about the beloved dialects of their grandparents. One young man offered that these ancient dialects represented the historical traditions of China, but there was no one to remember them. Where would China be without its historical legacy? Some other young women agreed -- they didn't want to lose the sound of these "grandmother" tongues, which brought back memories of their childhood, raised in rural villages by beloved elderly relatives. At the same time, they also sadly agreed that these rural dialects, like Ojibwe, probably were doomed. "No economic value" was a recipe for extinction in both cases. Again, bittersweet thoughts about the meaning of "progress" rose to the surface.

Some of the students addressed Native Americans, lost identities and "western lifestyles" on an exam when I asked what they had learned about the complex issue of "identity" in America. These were not topics exactly linked in the readings or class discussions, but their choice clearly reflected deep, personal connections:

One of the interesting things of studying American history is that it always reminds me of China. I still remember a photo took in a museum shows two Navajo artists are making a traditional pattern on the museum floor. These sacred patterns used to be an important part of their life but now it is only preserved and displayed in a museum. Their culture is doomed because there is no younger generation who recognize it and pass it on. Most Navajoes are modernized, or westernized. They eat, dress, talk like Westerners do but still they are Navajoes. In their veins flows the Navajo blood but the culture and traditions are gone. Similar identity crisis are happening to Chinese. More and more people start to celebrate Christmas instead of traditional ones like "Qing Ming" and "Duan W". We are gradually losing our identities as we go through the process of modernization.

Several other students commented as well on the corrosive force of "modernization" on both Native American and Chinese identity:

To those Chippewa who have adopted a western way of life, the things described in the songs, like the Sioux women, is totally strange to them, though they are ethnically Indian, the things that made them "Indian", or the Indian way of life had long disappeared. They simple can not find their cultural root. This puts the Indians in an awkward position where one leads a western way of life while he or she is an Indian, at the same time, though he or she is an Indian, his or her tradition is nowhere to be found.

It seems inappropriate that this question has been addressed twice in my homework, but I do think the very problem of the "loss of identity" is really being experienced by developing countries like China in the process of modernization, or, though we don't want to admit, in fact westernization.

As I looked around my class, it struck me that none of my students seemed to be fighting "westernization" very hard. I had never seen any of them wear traditional Chinese clothing, and they absolutely venerated American electronics. Nonetheless, it was clear from our study of this unit that my students felt like America in particular was "Western Expansion-ing" them. They didn't feel like Beijing was a threat to China's culture – more like New York. And again, this made for some pretty interesting lessons for me. Westward Expansion from the European perspective was, fittingly, our next topic.

The epoch of Westward Expansion began after 1862, when Congress passed the Homestead Act. If a citizen or intended citizen filed an application, then they could lay claim to one hundred and sixty acres of surveyed U.S. government land, live on the land and improve it for five years, and then file for outright title. This was the G.I. Bill of the mid-19th century in terms of extending opportunity to working-class Americans and new immigrants. And within two decades, a huge swath of the American West was "settled."

For homework on this topic, I assigned my students to read a group of letters written by the family of Uriah Oblinger, who moved from Indiana to Nebraska in the 1870s. A large collection of materials on this extended clan thankfully has been digitized and uploaded on the website of the Nebraska State Historical Society. The Oblinger letters describe yet another group of individuals worthy of empathy. They endured grueling journeys, money problems, crop failures, illness, death, intense homesickness, the discomfort of living in sod houses, and also the hope and optimism that led some to survive and prosper. On October 29, 1874, Uriah wrote to his family in Indiana:

> . . . after supper & lamp lit and table pulled up close to the stove as it is pretty cool & has been all day, spit a little snow this forenoon. it was pretty cold on my feet while carrying my pumpkins in the cellar this forenoon, as my boots are full of holes & cant wear socks in them will try and get a new pair when I sell my flax if I can get any thing for it. I carried my pumpkins in on my back as I have to be a pack horse now a days, but I am living in hopes of a team some day. . .

I also included a painting for them to look at – *American*

Progress by John Gast, which presented Westward
settlement as a glorified activity signified by an allegorical
symbol of Columbia. Gast presents America's national
"destiny" as a white, blonde, and scantily clad young woman
with the Star of Empire on her forehead and a schoolbook in
her hand, gliding west and leading a parade of pioneers (like
the Oblingers), and trains.

As much as my students empathized with the Native
Americans in the scene (fleeing progress as tiny figures on
the left side of the painting), once again they largely accepted
the settler point-of-view, and even found it inspiring:

> The great expansion has its deep root in American
> people's heart, for they believe it is their mission to
> bring democracy and freedom to as many places as
> possible. It is their "manifest destiny". The book
> represents the civilization the expansion would bring
> to the new west which includes cultivating the lands,
> establishing business and schools, having religion and
> traditions instead of the ways of living by the natives.
> We can see it from the painting in which it depicted
> different stages from primitive farming to modern
> transportation. This painting highlights the great
> success the American people have achieved through
> expansion and idealizes the image of America.

Another student expressed similar romantic appreciation for
the American "spirit" represented by the Oblingers, and
Gast's painting:

> First and foremost, the adventurous and risky spirit of
> these people encourage the coming generation of
> American people to keep working and creating which
> shapes the dynamic society today. this risky spirit
> also helps to explain the American people are so
> active and vigorous in creating things with giant
> companies such as Microsoft, Google, Apple, and etc.

A third student concurred, and extended the metaphor to an astute assessment of America's stance in the world:

> American society has a sense of mission and they put themselves in the role of "peacemaker" and "peacekeeper" in the world which can not separate from their Westward Expansion movement. The painting "American Progress" can give us an insight that it is their destiny to move Westward, to bring knowledge, freedom and democracy to the West. I think this movement deeply affect American people's sense of mission and the government's making foreign policy.

Surprisingly, this student did not see our assertiveness in the world as a bad thing (which I certainly had heard from others in China, as well as at home). Westernization and Expansion both seemed glorious to these students, even as they considered the very mixed story of cultural loss that our nation had presented.

To some extent, it was simply impossible to logically piece together the students' celebration of America's expansionist ideology, their appreciation for "doomed" older dialects and cultural traditions, and their fear of Westernization. Ultimately, though, this makes sense, because China's rising generation is transitional (and therefore confused) in so many different ways, just as our nation was in the late 19th century. In 1876, Native Americans were presented as uncivilized brutes, at the same time that their crafts were celebrated and reproduced at the Centennial Exposition, as well as increasingly in European-American homes throughout the country. My students similarly seemed to both venerate and scorn the rural village cultures many had emerged from. Further complicating matters was that they seemed to identify with both the winning and losing sides in the expansionist paradigm.

When I asked my students about their backgrounds, they usually told me that they considered themselves members of the vast umbrella majority group known as "Han" Chinese, but they also were Cantonese, and descended from grandparents who called themselves Hakka, Teoshew, Taishanese, or dozens of other Southern Chinese cultural groups. Thanks to their university education, the Internet, and Western influence in the "Reform and Opening Era," my students definitely were not similar culturally to their grandparents. All those parallels were directly applicable to America in the era we were studying.

In the process of our westward expansion, both Native Americans and European Americans were forced to leave behind much of what it meant to be Ojibwe, Sioux, Navajo, German, Irish, French, and hundreds of other distinct linguistic, religious, and ethnic traditions. Not all groups had a similar ability to control the pace and parameters of that change. Native Americans certainly didn't have the same choice as European immigrants like the Oblingers about where to live, or how much of their older identity to maintain. Dissecting these kinds of power differentials with students in America is critical to helping them understand the realities of history, as well as the present day.

In China, I got to be the student again, learning how power imbalances were shaping cultural change in this similarly dynamic era of fast-paced transition. On this theme, one of my students wrote her own "Lesson from America" in her final exam:

> First of all, I want to say something about "West Development," which was put forward by our government several years ago. This movement, which is similar to American "Westward Movement" to some extent, aims to develop the relatively impoverished areas in China. The painting

"American Progress" that John Gast painted tells us that we should consider all the advantages and disadvantages of this kind of movements, especially in treating the ethnic issue.

This student clearly took to heart the idealistic message embedded in projects like the efforts to preserve Ojibwe language. But she literally was the only one.

Like the Ojibwe, my academically successful "Han" students similarly had to choose between their ancestral identities, and their future "progress." Many told me that they had lost the ability to speak the languages their grandparents spoke – these had no economic value anymore, and the students were busy trying to master Mandarin, English, and dozens of other subjects they needed to get ahead. Most didn't visit their grandparents very often. On the rare occasions that conversation turned to the status of Cantonese in Hong Kong, or the dramatic protests of Tibetan Buddhists and other ethnic minorities, my students seemed fatalistic, just as most European Americans were in 1876. "Destiny" was inevitable, and unchangeable. It would be nice to think that our experience could be a cautionary tale rather than a playbook. But unfortunately, it seems like the Chinese government is bent instead on replaying a very sad old song, from its magisterial mountains in the Western provinces of Tibet, to Hong Kong's dramatic harbor, "white with foam."

Chapter Four. Wither Communism? The Gospel of Wealth and the Doctrine of Mao

As a teenager, I went through a phase of thinking that Communism was really awesome. When I was twelve, my family took advantage of the Great Recession of 1975 to buy an apartment in Manhattan. Over the summer following my graduation from elementary school, we moved from our sleepy middle class neighborhood in Queens, to a forty-three story apartment building on the Upper East Side. I had fortunately passed the entrance exam for admission to a public magnet school, and so my classmates were not kids from my ritzy new neighborhood, but instead from all five boroughs -- most from families with modest means. To say that Hunter College High School was liberal in those days would be a vast understatement. There were bake sales for the Southwest African People's Liberation Army, internships at the lefty radio station WBAI, and vigorous debates about which variety of radical liberalism was best. Almost everyone (with a few notable exceptions) thought that Ronald Reagan was evil.

New York City was not a great advertisement for the benefits of capitalism in the mid-1970s. Starkly contrasting scenes of incredible wealth – and incredible poverty – filled my days. It was an era in which you couldn't drive downtown without having homeless men and women dressed in rags try to "clean" your windows for donations at stoplights, while a few blocks away Michelin-starred restaurants served extravagant meals to the rich. Inequities like those shaped my opinion of capitalism as a sensitive adolescent -- basically, I thought it was terribly unfair for a rich nation to allow so many to go hungry. And so, I read Marx, and carried a copy of Mao's *Little Red Book* in my coat pocket. There had to be a better way.

My aversion to income inequality has stuck with me although, of course, my views have since been informed by further education, the *realpolitik* of adult life (mortgage, taxes, insurance, daycare and orthodontics expenses, etc.), and current events. The Berlin Wall crumbled while I was in graduate school, and it was hard to find much love for totalitarian regimes touting their empowerment of "the people" while jailing dissidents and restricting speech. Needless to say, after thirty-five years of thinking about politics and economics, I was intensely curious to know what my new "Communist" students thought about all these issues. I came up with what I thought would be a perfect test: what would they make of Andrew Carnegie, American capitalism's most ardent true believer?

Andrew Carnegie's story is of the "only in America" variety. He was born in Scotland in 1835, and immigrated to the United States in 1848 with his parents. Carnegie's father was a weaver put out of work by the Industrial Revolution, and so, as a child, he worked long hours in a bobbin factory and as a messenger boy, and eventually worked his way up in the ranks of a variety of companies from railroads to telegraphs.

In 1872, Carnegie read about an experimental new way to manufacture steel – the "Bessemer Process" – which drastically reduced the cost of the final product. The next year, funded by a group of partners and shareholders, he broke ground on his first steel plant on the shores of the Monongahela River outside Pittsburgh. The rest as they say, is history. Over the next two decades, Carnegie led the industry in introducing innovative new methods of production and delivery, and grew his business dramatically by building and acquiring other steel mills. In 1901, when he sold the Carnegie Steel Company to J.P. Morgan, the immigrant weaver's son became the richest man in the world.

Nineteenth-century "captains of industry" are generally pretty indefensible. They treated workers horribly, trashed the environment with wanton disregard, brutally suppressed unions and competitors, and often sported a "let them eat cake" kind of unattractiveness while they were building their gilded palaces and filling them with art (really great art, thankfully).

Carnegie is guilty of most of those things, but he is not entirely easy to write off as a moral sinkhole. After acquiring his phenomenal wealth, he gave away ninety percent of it -- in spectacular acts of philanthropy across the country, as well as in Scotland. His gifts included several university campuses, seven thousand organs for churches, and most famously sixteen hundred and seventy-eight public libraries across the United States -- complete with collections and endowments for ongoing support.

Reformers believed that libraries were the key to helping poor immigrants improve their prospects, and these new facilities typically offered English classes and free circulation of books to help other new Americans "pull themselves up by their bootstraps" -- as Carnegie had done. He also endowed significant and visionary organizations such as the Carnegie Foundation for the Advancement of Teaching, and the Carnegie Endowment for Peace. There is no question that he was a profoundly idealistic person, and in no way more so than in his attitude towards capitalism.

For their homework, I assigned my students to read a short but very influential essay Carnegie published in the *North American Review* in 1889. The title, very simply, was "Wealth" – later, it became known as "The Gospel of

Wealth." Its essential argument was that recent improvements in industry and innovation had created an inevitable, and unprecedented "difference between the dwelling, dress, food, and environment of the chief and those of his retainers. . . The contrast between the palace of the millionaire and the cottage of the laborer with us to-day measures the change which has come with civilization."

Under Carnegie's theory of wealth, income inequality (as it is known today) was a necessary element of modern society, because the law of competition between businesses inevitably meant that wages for workers would remain low. On the bright side, low wages would keep the price of commodities reasonable, so that in this great new world, "the laborer has now more comforts than the landlord had a few generations ago." The gap between "chiefs and retainers" would grow naturally within a Darwinian framework in which the "best man" would acquire wealth, and in doing so bring the entire "race" along with him.

The biggest shift in Carnegie's vision as compared with previous American dreamers – from Jefferson to Lincoln – was that there was little room or need for a middle class in this new "civilization." This was not presented as a problem, but rather as an inevitable and even desirable new American ideal:

> We accept and welcome therefore, as conditions to which we must accommodate ourselves, great inequality of environment, the concentration of business, industrial, and commercial, in the hands of a few, and the law of competition between these, as not only beneficial, but essential for the future progress of the race.

Lest we be concerned that such "concentration" in the hands of the few would be bad for everyone else, not to worry, because Carnegie had the answer: philanthropy. After

providing a model of "modest" living for oneself and
dependents, then the "man of Wealth" would act as the
"agent and trustee for his poorer brethren, bringing to their
service his superior wisdom, experience and ability . . ."

By 1889 when Carnegie published his essay, the
American Labor Movement already was well underway, and
there was no shortage of snarky criticism in response to his
"gospel." As an example, I also assigned a sarcastic version
of the "Lord's Prayer" written by a "workman" and
published in the *National Labor Tribune*:

> Oh, Almighty Andrew Philanthropist Library
> Carnegie, who art in America when not in Europe
> spending the money of your slaves and serfs . . . We
> bow before thee in humble obedience of slavery . . . If
> you sayest black was white, we believe you, and are
> willing, with the assistance of . . . the Pinkerton's
> agency, to knock the stuffing out of anyone who dares
> say you have been unjust in reducing the wages of
> your slaves . . . We love thee though our children are
> clothed in rags. We love thee though our wives . . .
> are so scantily dressed and look so shabby. But, oh
> master, thou hast given us one great enjoyment which
> man has never dreamed of before – a free church
> organ, so that we can take our shabby families to
> church to hear your great organ pour forth its
> melodious strains . . . Amen!

Finally, to round out the homework packet, I included photos
of the grand façade and palatial reading room of the New
York Public Library, which Carnegie referenced as one of the
grand illustrations of his thesis. From all these sources
combined, I thought I would glean a fantastic socialist-
communist critique of the evils of capitalism – and I did, but
the students' responses weren't entirely what I expected.

Among the many wrong assumptions I made about

my students, their political education was probably the most wrong. For example, I assumed that in all their many courses on "Political Ideology" they would have spent a lot of time reading the work of my adolescent hero. Karl Marx's most influential work was *Capital: A Critique of Political Economy*, published in 1867. For Marx, the essential evil of capitalism came in alienating laborers from the commodity-value of their work. Carnegie was a perfect example, because the people who produced the steel in his factories didn't earn anywhere near the value of their labor. The profit, instead, was alienated from the worker, and concentrated in the hands of the owner.

Because this alienation created an exploited worker class, Marx considered capitalism to be an inherently unstable system, and was joined in his beliefs by Vladimir Lenin and other influential philosophers and economists who followed him. Russian Communists adopted Marx's largely theoretical position, but added on an authoritarian twist. Since workers wouldn't necessarily choose to act in their own best interest (and for a variety of other reasons), government had to be controlled by a single party devoted to enforcing socialist principles. Hence, Communism was born as a single-party system of government.

Following in the footsteps of his Russian predecessors, Mao Zedong was intent on using revolution to operationalize socialist principles and form a Communist government in his own homeland. In China in the first half of the 20th century, the workers were agrarian and not industrial, but nonetheless the essential idea was the same – capitalism alienated workers from the value of their labor, and Communists would use revolution to destroy this exploitative system and root out its adherents in ensuing years. The Communist Party of China would represent workers, and organize society (and its educational systems) to support their interests.

It's hard to imagine that Andrew Carnegie and Mao Zedong could find any points of agreement. In his essay on "Wealth," Carnegie makes his own antipathy evident:

> The Socialist or Anarchist who seeks to overturn present conditions is to be regarded as attacking the foundation upon which civilization itself rests, for civilization took its start from the day that the capable, industrious workman said to his incompetent and lazy fellow, "If thou dost net [not?] sow, thou shalt net [not?] reap," and thus ended primitive Communism by separating the drones from the bees.

I expected that this would really irritate my students, and it did rankle some of them. One young woman wrote:

> A Workingman's "Prayer for the Masses" demonstrates laborers' rage against their miserable life in a capitalist society: they are enslaved by capitalism; they work hard but received little salary; they cannot even make their basic needs met and so on. Workingmen's terrible life sets such a striking contrast to the prosperous capitalist world.

And another student concurred:

> In the essay, Carnegie upholds the law of competition and thinks only the industrious man can prosper. So it seems that he is saying those poor people deserve to be poor because they are lazy. But as we know, labours in factories work at least twelve hours a day and appear to almost become a part of the machine on the assembly line. How can we say that they are lazy? If they are not lazy, why there seems to be no hope for them to become rich like their bosses?

This answer made a lot of sense to me – and it was exactly what I expected my Chinese students to take issue with. Even Western news coverage in the fall was filled with

reports of terrible working conditions and long hours at
Chinese factories (many of them making the latest electronic
devices for American consumers). And I knew that many of
my students had family members who worked in even worse
conditions for lower wages, in factories that didn't make it
into the spotlight.

Several other students similarly spoke up to defend
laborers against Carnegie's assessment, including another
perceptive young woman who noted that: "everyman wants
to be able to control their own fate. They want to pursue
whatever they like and live according to their own wills. But
in the capitalist society, their fate is at the mercy of those rich
capitalists like Carnegie."

While these students responded with the anti-
capitalist zeal I expected, I was surprised that just as many
thought capitalism was fine, but were skeptical about the idea
of philanthropy:

> The profit maximization and expanded reproduction
> are two principles of Capitalist economy, if all the fat
> cats spare their "surplus" wealth to nourish the public,
> no money could be devoted into production; then
> economy halts or even recedes.

This student seemed to be making the case that too much
philanthropy would weaken the economy, and so was
inadvisable.

Another student noted that Carnegie and his ilk would
be unable to make wise choices on behalf of those they could
never understand:

> Carnegie had made himself rich after experienced
> cruel commercial adventures and hardships, so he
> knew the significance of men's inner quality. He was
> distinguished and respectable business elite, but he
> was unable to jump out from the perspective of upper
> class and understand the situation of the working

class upon whose toil they built up the exploiting empire.

And a third student offered a similarly thoughtful but far less generous reflection on Carnegie's motives:

> [D]onating money for public projects is only an insidious way to suppress social discontent from the poor and to showcase their kindness. Finally, the public buildings, libraries, parks and so on built by capitalists are just more markers of their success and social contribution. Those buildings will stand forever even after their donors die so that they become the silent speakers of personal identity and success.

For this student, philanthropy only benefited the donor, and amounted to a version of "bread and circus" politics.

Personally, I love those fancy libraries. One of the greatest memories of my childhood is taking the bus down Fifth Avenue on Saturdays to spend the day doing homework in the grand reading room of the New York Public Library. The people-watching was as much fun as the treasure trove of books, journals, and bound portfolios delivered to the little window at the center of the cavernous space. Intense researchers pored over stacks of books, "bag ladies" sat at the long tables mumbling to themselves, and naptime for the elderly stretched on through much of the day. Women with no alternatives used the sinks in the creepy Ladies Room for impromptu sponge baths.

The building may not have served the exact purpose in those difficult years intended by its donors -- the Astors, Lenoxes, and Tildens – but it was definitely a huge benefit to everyone who strode past the magnificent lions to enter a cool marble oasis at the center of the city. The adorable little Carnegie libraries that dot the nation, even sometimes in the tiniest Vermont towns, are no less valuable in their own communities as well.

My students definitely did not share my romantic view of public libraries, perhaps because this is not the landscape of their youth as it is mine. One young man wrote:

> The New York Public Library looks magnificent yet behind it stands the enormous gap between the rich and the poor. While capitalists are rich enough to build grand buildings, workingmen cannot even make their basic needs met. And it is doubtful whether laborers can really benefit from the library. Is the library more of a showcase of social advance or a sarcastic sign of the evil derived from capitalism?

It never occurred to me to think of public libraries as evil, but I could definitely see his point.

In class, I reviewed my students' homework responses with them, and showed them photographs of many of the libraries built with Carnegie's money. I played devil's advocate as much as I could, but they didn't warm up too much to the idea of philanthropy. I don't think any of them will be carrying a copy of "The Gospel of Weath" in their pockets any time soon . . . but you won't catch them with Mao's *Little Red Book* either. The sad fact is that they don't think about politics very much. When pressed, my students confided that ideology was something they memorized for exams, and then tried to forget as quickly as possible. They don't talk about it for a lot of reasons – but mostly because it doesn't matter what they think, and they don't think it ever will.

On the whole, I learned a lot more about Chinese "communism" from this unit than they learned about American capitalism. Not one of them wrote anything favorable about their own political system in contrast to ours. There was not a reference to Marx, alienated labor, Mao's revolution, or anything like that, despite the many years they were required to study political science from a communist perspective. The truth is that they didn't even think about their country as the example of a "communist" ideological system.

On their final exams, several students came back to this topic in answering the question about what American history taught them about their own national experience. Reading these essays, I came to understand some just how much Carnegie's essay hit home – China home that is.

Another experience that Americans went through in the gilded age reminds one of what Chinese had during the economic reform and opening up period around 1987: the debate about wealth distribution in Andrew Carnegie's areas coincided with that of Chinese leader Deng Xiaoping's. To Carnegie, there is nothing wrong with wealth possessed by the capable rich as long as they benefit the poor by philanthropy. To Deng, some people should get rich ahead of others so that they can in return help the poor and a generally wealthy society can come into being. Both Carnegie and Deng believed in wealth possessed in proportion to individual effort and potential. Both are extremely positive about the rich assisting the poor but it should be noted that Deng's proposal met far less debates than Carnegie's.

As it turns out, my students didn't really differentiate Carnegie's theories from their own government, because the China they have grown up in has been much more closely aligned to Carnegie's Gospel of Wealth than Mao's *Little Red Book*.

What my students had a problem with was not China's turn towards capitalism, but rather their own deep, depressing cynicism about the ability or willingness of this government to act in the interests of the people. Capitalism is fine, but communist government officials (and their children), not so much:

> The administration of wealth of Carnegie, I think, just
> provides us Chinese wealth people a very persuasive
> and good example. With the dramatic economic
> growth these years in China, a large number of wealth
> people come into being. However, charity works and
> public donations seem not to be so popular.
> Reflecting upon this issue, several reasons are
> involved. First of all, people's trust on the
> government is extremely weak considering so much
> corruption and scandal from the government officials.
> For example, the scandalous news in China not long
> ago was that a young lady shows of her luxurious
> cars, bags and clothes proclaiming to be involved
> with the manager from the Red Cross. Thus, the
> donations of people drop dramatically. Secondly, the
> wealth people who started from scratch are still very
> cautious about their fortune. If China want to have
> more people like Carnegie, the transparency of the
> government should be established. And the trust
> between the government and its citizens should be
> reconstructed.

The conflict several of my students identified wasn't that
capitalism contradicted their own political ideals, but rather
that they distrusted government as a mechanism for sharing
wealth. They recognized their own government as an
exponent of Carnegie's "gospel;" for them, China's fast
trains, new bridges, and sleek expressways therefore carry
the same taint as my beloved childhood library. The
association many Chinese students of America made between
our Gilded Age and their present reality was amplified for me
a few months later.

Throughout the fall, I tried to establish connections
with the professors in the English department, but with little

success. Without the ability to read Chinese, I couldn't understand the campus e-mail system, and there wasn't much contact coming from my Dean, or any of the many administrators above me. Part of the problem simply was that the English faculty was moving out of a building about to be demolished to make way for a new classroom and office complex. Finally, at the end of the semester the dust had settled, and Fred and I were invited to our first major departmental event – a two-day retreat at which we humiliated ourselves singing KTV (Chinese karaoke) badly and suffered embarrassing defeat at Ping-Pong. We were in. I collected a lot of e-mail addresses from the lovely professors we met at the event, and prior to the start of the spring semester, I blanketed them with offerings of chats, lectures, research help, etc.

I was thrilled therefore, when early in February two young women professors in the department – Ying Mei and Cheng Li -- contacted me about teaching a faculty seminar. Both had studied and taught abroad, and they valued and missed taking part in Western-style seminars, and hoped I could lead one at GDUFS for interested faculty on Wednesday afternoons. To put the syllabus together, I asked that they poll the faculty and see what they were interested to learn more about, including topics on American history and culture, Western artistic traditions, and pedagogical techniques. Our initial list was a true hodgepodge, but it didn't really matter. Each week, the faculty who came peppered me with questions and comments, and brimmed with energy and enthusiasm – I told them that they were the best "students" I ever taught, and really, the whole thing was just incredibly fun.

One week, though, I messed up. We had been shifting the syllabus a bit from week-to-week as faculty proposed new topics, and on a Wednesday in mid-March I

loaded up my PowerPoint to a room full of heartbroken
faces. They thought I was going to discuss the Progressive
Era. Instead, I had prepared a lecture on the Architecture and
Culture of New York City. When I got to the architectural
superlatives of the gilded age Cheng Li burst out: "We know
we are living in our Gilded Age. Now we need a Progressive
Era. That is what I hoped you would tell us about!"

What she and some other faculty wanted, more
specifically, they told me, was an understanding of how
America got rid of the terrible conditions that existed in
America in the Gilded Age, and that characterize many
aspects of China today: government corruption; exploitative
banking practices; voter intimidation; bribery; suppression of
workers; corporate monopolies; vast income inequality;
unsafe food, transportation, drugs, and housing; poverty;
hunger; discrimination; and censorship. They knew about all
these problems from studying American history, most of
them abroad. I promised to fit the topic into a later lecture,
and moved on to the development of skyscrapers.

Two weeks later, I made up for my error by
delivering a lecture titled: "Efforts to Combat Inequality,
Poverty, and Corruption in America: From the Progressive
Era to the Great Society." I started with the Progressive Era
gains under Presidents Theodore Roosevelt (1901-1909) and
Woodrow Wilson (1913-1921). During these years from
1901-1919, the nation established income taxes; created the
Interstate Commerce Commission, Federal Trade
Commission, Food and Drug Administration, and the Federal
Reserve System; and began to enforce the Interstate
Commerce Act and Sherman Antitrust Act. I also made up
some bullet points demonstrating landmark legislation,
including: "1920 – 19th Amendment gives women the right to
vote." In this truly progressive period, public schools were
expanded dramatically; unions organized and began to

bargain effectively for higher wages, and cities like New York instituted civil service examinations for the promotion of municipal police and fire fighters, as well as more strenuous oversight of public employees.

I followed up by talking about the major achievements of Franklin Delano Roosevelt's New Deal and Lyndon Baines' Johnson's Great Society: the Social Security Act, Fair Labor Standards Act, and Securities and Exchange Commission (under Roosevelt); and the Transportation and Safety Administration, Medicaid, Medicare, Head Start, VISTA, and dozens of other anti-poverty programs (under Johnson).

As I was preparing for class, reviewing timelines and overviews on American history databases, I found it hard and sad to prepare to teach this subject. I knew from Cheng Li's outburst that she wanted me to tell her how a progressive era could happen in China, but in truth, all the gains that were made depended on tools China doesn't have: grassroots campaigns, an independent judiciary, a (meaningful) Bill of Rights, and especially freedom of speech and of the press to document and call out corruption, inhumane conditions, etc. I could explain what happened and how activists won tough battles, but it was hard to see how these American lessons could apply in a country with none of the above. Ida Tarbell, whose investigative journalism led to the dismemberment of Standard Oil, and Lewis Hine, whose photographs documented child labor in appalling conditions, probably would be imprisoned in China today.

Instead, in rich provinces like Guangdong, China looks a lot like Carnegie's ideal, with vast concentrations of wealth in the hands of a few, and hundreds of millions of poorly-paid workers – thoroughly alienated from the commodity-value of their labor. In fact, walking around the streets of the financial district in Guangzhou feel that much different than the unequal landscape of my childhood.

Although the bullet points about the Progressive Era and Great Society look really great on the screen, in fact we are different from China in many ways only by degree. At the end of the class, I showed them headlines from that week's *New York Times* regarding hunger, corruption, and lax regulatory oversight in America, all of which demonstrated that the work was far from over. Nevertheless, the history of the various movements was fairly compelling. In many eras of our history, Americans have come together to try and craft a "more perfect union." The question is, can China?

In 1989, Deng Xiaoping coined the phrase "socialism with Chinese characteristics" to describe his new political theory, but in reality, it's hard to see socialism in operation in China today. In the ritziest areas of Guangzhou, horribly deformed people are laid out across the sidewalks by family members, with bowls for contributions, while the luxury vehicles of China's new millionaires (and billionaires) buzz by. Range Rovers, BMWs, Porsches and Ferraris are a common sight, as are swanky restaurants serving expensive delicacies like shark's fin and jumbo crabs. Meanwhile, on the outskirts of town, the poor grow food along roadsides, and in fields bulldozed to make way for new developments they will never be able to afford. Many rich Chinese find ways to move their wealth outside of the Mainland – taking their fortunes with them, far from the workers who created it in the first place. Karl Marx would be appalled.

Once again, I was reminded of the New York of my childhood – the kid whose parents bought out the QE2 for his bar mitzvah, the crazy prices paid for trophy paintings by Van Gogh and Monet, and the Roman orgies of food and spectacle carried on often just steps from desperately sad cases of homelessness and illness. This is not exactly the America Carnegie envisioned, but it is the America his

"Gospel" promised. Today, his theory seems to be just as much alive, or maybe even moreso, in China, the country-formerly-known-as-communist.

Chapter Five. The People's Republic of Censorship

My two most visceral experiences of censorship in China occurred while lecturing in Shenzhen in the winter, and then again on vacation in Hong Kong in early summer, 2012. In the first instance, an American professor on faculty at a university in Shenzhen abruptly ended an invited guest lecture on the history of American censorship when I brought up a slide with a still shot of Roberto Rosselini's movie "The Miracle," which shows a naked female angel provocatively straddling a naked man. Her breasts are visible, but that's about it. In 1952, the United States Supreme Court for the first time ruled that motion pictures like Rosellini's fell under the category of protected expression, and not regulated commercial speech -- the case is hugely important in the history of first amendment rights.

Nonetheless, the American professor in Shenzhen pronounced quite smugly that the image was not fit for his graduate students, and he was going to have to adopt the posture of Anthony Comstock, the censor I previously had discussed. Regardless of my pique, his actions were a perfect example of my lecture points, as the students in attendance were left to wonder what happened in the remaining historical periods included in my presentation. Censorship results in ignorance.

The situation was intensely awkward, as students rushed into the hallway to apologize following my dismissal, and hurriedly signed a card thanking me for coming. Their English professor had made them lose face – and embarrass a

guest – which no Chinese professor would have done. A few
of them asked me for a copy of the PowerPoint, but I didn't
want to give it to them for fear of causing more trouble with
the professor. His act of censorship, as much as I disagreed
with it, undeniably caused a "chilling effect."

My second most visceral experience of censorship
was less personally dramatic, but far more telling of the
Orwellian virtual reality China has tried to create for itself
through censorship. On our way home at the end of the
academic year, we stayed for a week in Hong Kong– one last
stay in this beloved city, with its intoxicating mix of natural
beauty and historic complexity, felt palpably as we rode on
century-old ferries and cable cars. The aromas of roasting
ducks; frying chili crabs; fragrant ginger, garlic, and spices;
and occasionally rotting garbage all combined for a
hedonist's nirvana.

Although we were there mostly for last bowls of great
noodles before leaving Asia, we happened to be in town for
the fifteenth anniversary of Britain's return of Hong Kong to
China. President Hu Jintao flew in from Beijing, and as a
result the streets of Central, near our hotel, were filled with
protestors. They were angry about the "election" of Leung
Chun-Ying, the new Chief Executive for Hong Kong –
believed to have too-close ties with the Communist Party--
and they protested against restraints on civil liberties and
suppression of dissidents on the Mainland. An added irritant
was Leung's decision to deliver his inauguration speech,
facing Hu Jintao, entirely in Mandarin, despite the fact that
Hong Kong residents overwhelmingly prefer Cantonese or
English.

The local Hong Kong television stations and
newspapers covered the protests extensively, running hours
of video showing streets filled with tens of thousands, if not
hundreds of thousands of protestors. But in China, the papers

made no mention of the protests, and the state-sponsored CCTV jumped from coverage of speeches in a palatial auditorium to the harbor fireworks that night. The *China Daily News* included this synopsis:

> The local community gave a positive response to the president's three-day visit, with many convinced that the central government's backing and economic incentives for Hong Kong would benefit the city in the long run. "President Hu's words show that he cares about Hong Kong, its people and the city's progress and development, and he wants all Hong Kong people to reap the fruits of its success," said Kei Shek-ming, a veteran current affairs commentator. Ashley Wong, a 13-year-old student, told China Daily that she is proud and happy with the achievements Hong Kong has made in so many fields since the handover.

It's always just a "typical day in the neighborhood" as far as the *China Daily News* is concerned.

Although Article 35 of China's constitution states that: "Citizens of the People's Republic of China enjoy freedom of speech, of the press, of assembly, of association, of procession and of demonstration," nobody in their right mind here pretends that those words carry any real meaning. In fact, if you search for the term "free speech China" using Chinese servers, you are likely to come up with a "can't open the page" message. In daily activity on the Internet in China, the "can't open the page" message comes up a lot.

As many other analysts have noted, the "Great Firewall" is about as effective today as the Great Wall was hundreds of years ago at keeping Mongolians out – in other words, not effective at all. It is true that for the hundreds of millions who don't bother trying to get around the wall, the Internet is remarkably censored. American sites like

Facebook, YouTube, Twitter, the Chronicle of Higher Education, Dropbox, and Google Docs all are routinely blocked, and sites referencing controversial topics such as dissident artist Ai Weiwei, imprisoned writer Liu Xiaobo, Tiananmen Square, Tibet, the names of corrupt Chinese officials, etc., also come up with the "can't open the page" response.

According to my friends in Guangzhou, the situation is much worse for those using the Internet in Chinese. Tens of thousands of censors (and possibly more than that) work for the government, blocking newly sensitive search terms as they arise. A Carnegie Mellon study of Sina Weibo (Chinese Twitter) in 2012 reported that 50% of Tibetan messages, and about 12% of Beijing and Shanghai messages were removed by censors.

In the place of actual news, you will find a steady stream of statements agreeing with whatever policy the government is currently advertising. Reportedly, a huge number of Chinese are paid to post pro-government sentiments on social media sites as part of the "50 Cent Army" (as in 50 cents per post). Independent journalists not on the team who report on Chinese government actions in a negative way (there are a lot) routinely are expelled or denied visas if they are foreign -- or much worse if they are local. One of my undergraduate students told me that she was going to study journalism in Hong Kong instead of China. "Even though it's more expensive," she said, "it's actually journalism. If you study that in China, it's just public relations."

Despite the ominous sound of all of this, in practice, getting around censorship is simple for English-speaking expats with credit cards, and a daily, only somewhat annoying cat-and-mouse game for my Chinese colleagues and students. For our part, we were able to avoid Chinese censors from our first week on the mainland, simply by installing a VPN (virtual private network) on our computers, smart phones and iPad. If a site was blocked, all we needed to do was activate the VPN, and within seconds we were searching freely via unfiltered servers in Los Angeles, Las Vegas, Chicago, Tokyo, or Paris. Graham had our VPN up and running for a small fee in just a couple of hours.

Getting around censors seems to be something of a "Don't Ask, Don't Tell" arrangement for the Chinese. Some people told me that they fear the heavy penalty if they are caught using a VPN, and/or they don't have the credit card numbers to buy one, or the knowledge to set one up. However, my students didn't seem to have any problem at all. One student showed me a website he could go to that sent his searches out through a proxy server – we tried "Hu Jintao corrupt" to see what would happen – and boom, we were over the wall. He said that these websites get shut off frequently, but students always find another one to go to. He also told me he wasn't aware that this was illegal.

Even without inside knowledge of the right web addresses, the people I spoke with reported finding lots of ways to get information about current events on popular micro blog sites using an elaborate system of code words. If "Jasmine revolution" is blocked, it will soon be signified using a new term. The word spreads with a cyber nod and wink, and the conversation continues. This system doesn't seem hard for Chinese insiders to figure out, and I was always surprised at how much my students and colleagues knew about persecution of dissidents, worker uprisings, corruption cases, Tibetan self-immolations, etc., that clearly were on Beijing's list of heavily-censored topics. These controversies were never discussed in public, but they would come up in private conversations with no one else around, or during the fairly freewheeling "American" dinners we held frequently in our apartment.

After raising this issue with a friend on campus, however, she took the time to send me her own take on the subject of Internet censorship – and to point out that it had a long history in Chinese society.

> Looking back on Chinese history, ups and downs of the dynasties are quite similar--groups of people launching revolutions, taking over power, and losing power to other groups of people. The communist party has flourished no more than a century. The party leaders, like any leaders with imperial power, know how important it is to calm people down, restrict them and make them less likely to create upheavals. In history, there was an infamous method to reach that end--literary inquisition. I think internet censorship today inherits some traits of that. When people regularly face difficulty to discuss about politics freely, some might just give up eventually. However, the idea that Chinese people as a whole do not talk about politics is wrong. Ostensibly, Chinese people are afraid of being too aggressive in political discussion, but in daily chitchat, people always complain about policies and wrongdoings of the government. Many people speak ill of the party, but of course not as much online.

Her comments helped me to understand the response of my Chinese students and lecture audiences to this subject. Censorship hadn't stopped them from being critical – it just resulted in modes of expression that were less likely to cause trouble. In contrast, Americans generally are much less afraid of "being too aggressive in political discussion," as our television and radio news shows routinely demonstrate. My lectures on censorship, once again, served as an opportunity to demonstrate how Americans publicly address uncomfortable subjects.

Teaching censorship can be a tricky business anywhere, because most suppressed culture makes people uncomfortable in some way. In the case of the United States, understanding our history of censorship requires, among other things, looking at erotic images that at some point have been classified as "obscene" -- like the still from Rosselini's movie.

When I received notification that I had been awarded a Fulbright Scholar grant to teach in China, I was of course honored, but also somewhat surprised. In my application, I discussed my research on the history of censorship, and my desire to see how it influenced Chinese culture. In the months after I submitted my application, Tahrir Square in Cairo filled with protesters, a wave of revolutionary activity spread across the globe, and China responded by vastly increasing its already gargantuan censorship infrastructure. My friends in America joked that I would land in jail if I went to China to talk about censorship. All of us just assumed that my application would be turned down, hence the surprise when it was instead approved.

Once I got to China though, it became pretty clear that I didn't need to be worried about jail. In fact, I was a pretty insignificant fly swimming in a lot of ointment, and foreigners in general (especially in relatively liberal Guangdong Province) are given much more leeway than nationals in the area of free speech. As the Fulbright staff reminded me (and as I reminded myself over the course of the year), I was not a China expert – I would teach what I know about American history and culture, and my audience could draw connections with their own experience in any way they liked.

This situation created an enormous opportunity for me -- not only to hone and test theories of censorship I had been developing in my scholarship -- but also to open discussions with Chinese students and professors that they rarely if ever held in public. In fact, "Censorship of Visual Culture in the United States" was by far the most requested lecture on my circuit. I delivered this ninety-minute speech in Shantou, Nanjing, Hong Kong, Shenzhen (about half of it, anyway), Guangzhou, and Qingdao – typically to large crowds – with at least thirty minutes of vibrant Q and A following. Audience members typically expressed surprise that we had any tradition of censorship whatsoever, and asked questions such as "how could there be so much censorship in a free country?" "why is America so much more afraid of sex than European countries?" and "what do you think of censorship in China?" Overall, the response to my academic discussion of the mechanisms, targets, and history of censorship in America was consistent in venues across the country. Students and professors I met in the People's Republic – among the most censored people in the world – are at least as stridently and unanimously pro-free speech as Americans.

Because I was trained as an art historian, I am especially interested in the effects of censorship on visual culture. The lecture I delivered in China on this subject, therefore, covered what I know best: the regulation of photographs, paintings, films, video games, performance art, the Internet, etc. from 1630 to the present. Before I got started on this vast overview, however, I started with a series of introductory slides to help frame the discussion. The most important one, obviously, simply read:

THE FIRST AMENDMENT OF THE U.S. CONSTITUTION
Congress shall make no law respecting an *establishment of religion*, or prohibiting the free exercise thereof; or *abridging the freedom of speech*,

or of the press; or the right of the people peaceably to
assemble, and to petition the government for a redress
of grievances.

The italicized phrases, I pointed out, were the tricky parts.
"Make no law respecting an establishment of religion"
presumes that legislators and courts can determine easily
when a law violates this principle, and can scrupulously
maintain secular laws in a society in which people hold
strong religious beliefs.

No law "abridging the freedom of speech" is also a
pretty tough standard to uphold -- some abridgments are
always necessary for the safety and health of a community.
If I make a serious and direct call for assassination, or yell
"fire" in a crowded theater, my words constitute a threat to
the life and liberty of others, and as such, that speech is
illegal, even in the United States. On the flip side, we endure
a tremendous amount of hateful and hurtful speech for the
sake of an ideal; to put it mildly, the First Amendment's
broad principles are not easy to live up to.

My next two slides set the terms of the discussion on
an academic, intellectualized plain, and gave students in the
audience a yardstick against which to judge their own
experiences. The first listed the *Academic American
Encyclopedia's* definition of censorship:

> . . . suppression of information, ideas, or artistic
> expression by anyone . . . It may take place at any
> point in time, whether before an utterance occurs,
> prior to its widespread circulation, or by punishment
> of communicators after dissemination of their
> messages, so as to deter others from like expression.

This broad definition reflects the fact that the vast majority of
censorship happens "before an utterance occurs," when
people choose not to speak – often because of the fear
generated by witnessing the punishment of others. Whether

censorship is enforced by a policeman with a weapon, or is self-inflicted in response to someone else's oppression, the effect on speech is the same.

My final slide of "important terms" also helped to clarify the full landscape of abridgments, both at home and out in the world:

MECHANISMS OF CENSORSHIP

Direct Actions – including prosecution, legislation, seizure and destruction of materials

Indirect Actions – financial and other forms of pressure, procedural and regulatory controls, religious and social sanctions

Self-Censorship – individual decisions to restrain speech due to awareness of potential actions

People tend to think of the first category – "Direct Actions" as the only one that counts. But as I point out, financial and procedural controls can have similar effects. A museum under pressure to please its corporate sponsors may choose not to show politically controversial or critical work. Likewise, municipalities may permit the "freedom" to assemble and petition government for "redress of grievances" – but if the fees for sanitation, police services, etc., required to hold a march or protests are set at a prohibitive rate, then you really only have as many freedoms as you can pay for.

Following these introductory concepts, I divided the story of American censorship into five historical periods. From 1630 to 1873, images were regulated almost entirely within the private spheres of churches and homes. The second period covered the years from 1873 to 1915, when government censorship was at its height under the reign of Anthony Comstock. Comstock was an evangelical Christian who lobbied Congress to pass tough censorship laws in 1873, with the backing of wealthy supporters. As a result of these efforts, he was appointed to serve as a postal inspector, and empowered to enforce American morals as the nation's first federal censor with the power to prosecute.

During his forty-two years of service, Comstock's haul of "obscenities" included more than four million photographs, prints, newspapers, books, birth control devices, and pamphlets on sexual health (including most famously Margaret Sanger's *Family Limitation*). By the time of his death in 1915, Comstock's actions had resulted not only in vast seizures and arrests, but also in a strong backlash that included the creation of organizations passionately committed to suppressing him, and expanding the scope of first amendment protections. Although the bitter pain he inflicted on his victims is undeniable, overall I would contend that no individual in American history has done more to expand free speech rights. Comstock proved beyond the shadow of a doubt that censorship was both un-Constitutional and profoundly ineffective.

In the third section of my talk, I outlined the history of court cases and legislative shifts that vastly expanded the scope of first amendment protections between 1915 and 1980. Each case demonstrated how increasingly explicit content and themes were deemed to fall under the category of 'protected speech' with 'redeeming social value.' On the night the X-rated film *Midnight Cowboy* won the Oscar for Best Picture in 1969, Comstock undoubtedly rolled over in his grave.

The final sections of my talk covered the hostile standoff between politicians, artists, and curators that characterized the 1980s, and then the new technologies and present conditions of culture and censorship in the United States. My final bullet points provided a glossy summary:

- Private Internet connections in the United States are not subject to censorship, except in the case of child pornography. However, businesses and government offices may use filtering software at their discretion, and public schools and libraries are required to do so if they wish to receive federal telecommunication funds.

- Indirect forms of censorship, such as economic difficulties in funding provocative work, are quite common, but direct forms of censorship of visual culture are quite uncommon.
- The United States legal system has struggled to apply the First Amendment, and older censorship laws, to new technologies.

The first two of these bullet points describe a situation almost completely opposite that in China. The third is a challenge that every government now faces, and that promises to be especially difficult in countries that really want to control information. My audiences throughout China all agreed – nobody thought that CPC censors could keep up with the explosive expansion of the Internet, and especially the incredible popularity of micro blogging, which pokes billions of holes each day in the not-so-Great-Firewall.

In addition to delivering this lecture for my students at GDUFS, I also assigned them to read an article I had written for *Common-Place Journal* called "Searching for Smut." The article details my archival hunt for surviving examples of the materials censored under Anthony Comstock's reign. One of my graduate students remarked with great savvy that: "it seems like your research is a form of protest against censorship since you are trying to undo what the censor did."

The most common response to my article confirmed the sentiments I had heard around the country: censorship was not accomplishing its intended purpose. A young man wrote:

Firstly, it is impossible to completely erase these so

called obscene products, which could be proven by the facts occurring in the process of Comstock's practices. There existed many survivors escaping his censor. That is exactly the case as same as that happened in Qin Dynasty that, most of the books the emperor wanted to burn survived from the persecution. Secondly, the criterion that Comstock employed was questionable. He just destroyed the products that "he thought" were obscene. And he was a typical puritan, but the question is that people cannot judge all the things under the old and traditional puritan doctrines. Finally, such actions are overcompensating. The existing things always get their reasons to exist. Just take prostitution for example. For centuries people have always been struggling to wipe out the prostitution, only to find it grows faster and wider. So what we should do and only can do is to face the facts and set up necessary regulations rather than fruitlessly trying to destroy them.

While this student saw censorship as largely impotent, another young woman saw it instead as a grave impediment to the development of a national conversation about morality. She posed an interesting question for her homework: "For a nation, what is more important, virtue or freedom of speech?"

In my opinion, for a nation, freedom of speech comes first. Free speech, discussion and debate can only bring out a clearer view of what is really good and what is evil. On the contrary, suppressing different voices only leads to more doubt, curiosity and reaction. Therefore, in spite of Comstock's fervent hunting down "indecent" and "obscene" matters, America is not saved from the dangers of obscenity. On the other hand, the insistence of virtue, in many cases, tends to easily go to the extreme and destroy what is good while clearing out the undesired. The enormous volume of great paintings and books censored are the victims of Comstock's purifying crusade. Therefore, although honest and free speech may cause chaos and uncertainty in the short run, it will gradually and eventually sort out the truth and at the same time, avoid strangling the possible good.

A third student offered a similar, bitter diatribe against the effects of censorship that clearly referenced Chinese experience as much as American:

To me, establishing a national line means repression and dictatorship and it is surely a disaster for the creating of the art. It is obvious that Anthony Comstock tries to exert his Puritanical conservativeness and esthetics into every one's mind and even the execution of law so that he can save the fallen souls of American people. What he does is not something heroic, ambitious or even mature, but rather a dreadful move exclusive of any other possibility, leaving no space for imagination or any inventive thought . . . As Justice Anthony M. Kennedy wrote, "*First Amendment freedoms are most in danger when the government seeks to control thought or to justify its laws for that impermissible end. The right to think is the beginning of freedom, and speech must be protected from the government because speech is the beginning of thought.*"

Once the national line is drawn on the morality as a standard for people to create an artistic work, superficiality is inevitable. What people care about is the form, not the essence; the outward shape, not the corn idea. If so, we may never have the chance to appreciate those unconventional and bold artistic works any more, which is truly a disaster for art.

This phrase describing the effects of censorship – the "outward shape, not the corn idea" -- struck me as especially perceptive. In years of researching censorship, I had never thought about it in those terms. But it explained so much about China, and every country that imposes government censorship on its people.

As in the case of China's coverage of Hu Jintao's visit to Hong Kong, what censors almost always accomplish is just to put a mask over the underlying reality – rather than actually changing culture or morals. Comstock's tireless efforts didn't reduce in any way the popularity of obscenity in America. His own arrest blogs demonstrate that point amply; he never was able to nab more than a small trickle in a great stream of American smut. His efforts simply resulted in a shift in how these materials were distributed. In China also, people don't stop talking about censored scandals, corruptions, protests, etc., they just use an increasingly sophisticated array of code words and technological pathways for communication. In both cases, government censors can report how much speech they are stopping, but not how much they are spurring in new venues through their efforts. And Hong Kong is still filled with angry protestors, whether the Chinese government wants to acknowledge that or not.

The issue of "outward shape" came up in another exchange I had with a student, regarding the party pronouncements English students often practice translating for homework:

> As I see it, Chinese political speeches are always filled with cliches--eulogies of the party, revolutions, the Reform and Opening Up. You can always hear "improve", "sustain", "uphold", and "achievements"--

which are very empty words. It's not that politicians have nothing to talk about, but the positive phrasing of the speech will never trigger any political controversy. They simply fear to talk about controversial topics--such as Tibet self-immolation-- and once a controversy is raised, they will struggle to seal people's mouths. Once the communist party was so keen on revolutions, but now anything that might detonate a revolution can make party leaders freak out. Hence there are empty talks, fake positiveness, and seeming harmony.

"Seeming harmony" doesn't do anything to change the reality of the situation, in Hong Kong, Tibet or anywhere else. What it does accomplish is to make people in China incredibly cynical about everything their government says. They know they aren't seeing a true picture, but instead only a constructed alternate universe.

Many of my students chose to write about Comstock for the final exam question in which I asked them to share what they had learned about China from America's historical experience. They took different lessons from the unit, but once again confirmed my initial impression – the attitudes towards censorship that I experienced in China were overwhelmingly bitter, angry, and cynical. And, as in America's historical example, the students knew a lot about things they weren't supposed to know anything about. One student wrote:

With the pass of Comstock Act, Comstock became the emperor to censor and destroyed what was "bad." Thus tons of books, paintings, etc. including excellent works from great artists fell into his preys. This event reminds one of Chinese Cultural Revolution between 1966 and 1976. Due to Mao Zedong's aim of purifying the socialist China, artists were persecuted, arrested, and accused of anti-socialism and tormented to death with their fantastic works set on fire or destroyed in other ways. China seemed to pay a higher price, but the lesson is the same: freedom of speech (in art in these two cases) should never fall into one single law, and when it does, damages are irreparable.

The Cultural Revolution was an especially fitting example to use in a discussion of censorship because the entire decade is covered in a single page in Chinese high school textbooks.

Rather than openly confront the most painful episodes of Communist history, the government routinely chooses to prohibit discussion of such topics, in art, film, or literature, and especially in educational settings. The Cultural Revolution came up in another final exam response as well:

Similarly, China also has invisible "Comstock" who censored films and many films not allowed to release in China mainland such as "To Live" directed by Yimou Zhang is widely accepted by critics and to me is an excellent one. The reason is that this movie reflect people's life during the Culture Revolution which seems to violate the principle of the Chinese government and destruct the image of China. I think the value of movies cannot be decided by government or anyone who has power. Any regulation or limitation on this would damage the artists' enthusiasm and passion to innovate new artistic works.

As an art historian and free speech advocate, all I could say to this was simply "Amen." What I didn't say to my students during my year in China, because it just was too painful and unhelpful, was just how much I knew censorship was damaging their future prospects in ways they could not imagine. The impact of government censorship on their lives goes far beyond damage to artistic enthusiasm, passion, and innovation.

Three days a week, I held office hours in a starkly bright and empty room titled the "Foreign Teacher Office," up four flights of stairs in "Building 7." There were four desks in the room, but I rarely saw anyone else use them. The building had been newly renovated, so there was an air conditioner unit, and a steady supply of hot water for tea. The porcelain trench toilets in the WC down the hall were not my preference, but they were rarely used and extremely clean compared with the classroom areas. As usual, this was a no-soap-or-toilet-paper facility, which required inelegantly strolling down the corridor with my own supply.

Students sometimes seemed surprised when they found me at my desk in the empty room with blank white walls – they were not used to visiting professors for open office hours. Once settled in though, these one-on-one meetings were always enjoyable. My undergraduate students typically came just to chat about random topics and practice their English. In the fall, a particularly soft-spoken, lovely young woman entertained me for over an hour by pointing out the major cities and sites in Guangdong Province on a map. I wish I could have recorded her soothing voice for those nights I have trouble sleeping, but fortunately I managed to stay awake during her entire visit. She was happy to have the opportunity to practice her English for so long.

My graduate students typically did not stop by just to chat – instead, they were there with a purpose. As majors in English Language and Culture, they were eager to get more English-language sources for my course assignments, as well as for their thesis papers. The University library had few academic books or journals on American topics, and getting books from America was far too costly and difficult. The databases available on the University website were limited, and downloading articles was painfully slow. In our meetings together, I was able to login to my Saint Michael's College library databases easily, and locate citations to suitable articles they were excited to read.

Unfortunately, downloading these articles as .pdf files was practically impossible on campus. Sometimes, using the VPN sped up the process; avoiding the censors had the collateral benefit of avoiding the inevitable bandwidth problems that result when everyone's requests have to squeeze through a filtered pipeline. Nevertheless, the process still was painfully slow, and I ended up on many occasions downloading articles for them overnight in my apartment.

It is difficult – if not actually impossible – to teach advanced critical thinking without access to research. In America, my students have unlimited access to sources at lightning speed. Professional reference librarians are on duty to help them navigate the wealth of nations available to them, on campus, online, and through interlibrary loan. Our nation's college and university libraries are testaments to our thirst and love for new knowledge. In China, I had to reduce the research requirement for my students to just two sources, because there was so little we could get – either in the library or on the Internet. Without my VPN and library website from home, I probably would have eliminated the requirement for research from my courses altogether. The practical result of China's censorship policies for its students is that they are running a race to the global knowledge economy of the future with (proverbial) balls and chains attached to their legs. You really can't teach critical thinking skills like that, even if you really want to.

When our friend Keith came from America to visit us, I took him to visit the amazing new library just opening in Zhujiang New Town. I describe this stretch of Guangzhou built for the 2009 Asian games as 23rd century – not 21st. There is Zaha Hadid's impressive and challenging Opera House, across from an athletic stadium out of a Transformer's movie, and across from that the massive new public library, beautifully designed by the Japanese firm Nissen Sekkei. As we walked through the open doors, the impressive scale of the building overwhelmed us; it gives great face. But after nearly ten months, there were still practically no books on the shelves. I thought about what it would take to fill up that vast space, given the Chinese government's restrictive attitudes towards information.

It's not just that speech is un-free in China – it's that the official attitude towards knowledge is the opposite of our own. Knowledge isn't power in China – it's peril. The "corn ideas" – those beautiful kernels of unwashed, uncooked essential seeds of education – can only be de-husked by those who are not afraid of new knowledge. When people live in a society permeated by fear of direct actions of censorship, they inevitably respond with self-censorship. If the new library is anything like the library on the GDUFS campus, it will be filled only with texts that don't risk peeling back any of the protective layers on the face of Chinese culture. What a shame -- but also a lesson for me about the deeper functions of censorship in any society.

The "face" of the new library looks fantastic. What goes into it clearly will be a secondary consideration. Anything deemed remotely critical of the Party, or injurious to "public morals," will be excluded. If you read through (and believe) the information on offer, you will think the Communist party is simply fantastic. And that's a big, human element of the impetus for censorship.

When I try to teach my kid to use polite language, it's not only because he's going to hopefully have better success in society – but also, he's going to make me look good as a parent in front of his teachers, my neighbors, family, etc. Like an insecure parent, the Communist party has a thin skin when it comes to criticism. What it fails to understand is that increased censorship is not a sustainable or harmless answer to the problems of growing unrest.

The CPC's well-advertised prosecutions and persecutions encourage the nation's librarians, professors, and students not only to tolerate direct and indirect forms of censorship, but also to constantly engage in self-censorship, none of which is conducive to the professed goal of global competitiveness. The corn ideas simply can't grow without sunlight. My students in China don't have a prayer of seriously competing with my students in America unless their government gives up its anti-intellectual, ineffective, expensive, and inevitably doomed censorship campaigns.

Course Two: America in the 1960s

In the same manner that our 19th century sheds light on China's present, our 1960s may predict its future. China's challenges include increasingly vocal protests, social upheaval, and a rising (internet-saturated) generation with the luxury of dreaming about systemic change.

Chapter Six. "The Ballot, or the Bullet:" The Question of Political and Social Change in China

Overall, it wasn't a great year for the CPC, with unrest and unhappiness pretty much a constant in hot spots across China. In the fall and winter of 2011, thousands of protestors occupied municipal offices and stormed the streets to protest land seizures and official corruption in the small coastal village of Wukan, not too far from GDUFS in Guangdong province. Security agents from the government abducted five leaders of the protests, and one of them, Xue Jinbo, died in police custody, thus prompting even more protests. Wukan was not alone; Bloomberg News reported that expenditures on police enforcements in China for 2011 indicated that there had been approximately 180,000 such "mass incidents" to quell in that year. Wukan was an exaggerated example, but not especially unusual. Overall, it's hard to overstate the problems faced by the CPC in maintaining control as it pursues "progress" without the consent of the governed.

Dissenters come in a wide variety of flavors in China, from those who speak out on a grand stage, to those who commit small acts of resistance on social media. The outspoken celebrity artist Ai Weiwei uses constant uploads of pictures, videos, tweets, and exhibition of innovative art works to broadcast his complaints and persecutions internationally from Beijing. Less famous dissidents crop up on social media on a regular basis, like "Guy X," who investigates corruption and posts detailed accusations on his micro blog; and Deng Jiyuan, whose wife was forced to have an abortion in her seventh month of pregnancy because the family couldn't pay the fine for a second child. Deng posted a photo of his wife and aborted baby lying in a hospital bed on social media and the image 'went viral,' eliciting rage against the officials involved, as well as many posts (some perhaps from the "fifty cent army") calling Deng a "traitor" for taking his story to the media, where it was picked up by foreign journalists. My students consistently knew all about these stories, even though they were not mentioned in the mainstream media.

Interested parties around the world, from journalists, to diplomats, to bankers, watch all of this closely and debate the same questions. How much longer can China's Communist government use repressive tactics and continue to lead, and survive? Can it censor its way out of unrest? Can it keep the peace when the economy inevitably slows? Will it be able to control unruly borderlands like Tibet and Hong Kong, and the artists of Beijing, without sparking revolution? Can the party control its own corruption and infighting to continue on a path of progressive reform and avert these other potential disasters?

These questions are feverishly debated in board rooms and class rooms across the West, but the answers won't come from there. They will come from the world's most important rising generation – today's post-Cultural Revolution, technology-laden Chinese youth. What will they expect and demand? How will they behave in the face of repression and a feeling of powerlessness as they come of age? The closest I came to enlightenment on these subjects came from a semester teaching "Introduction to American Studies: The 1960s," about our own great and terrible era of change, led by young people.

My 1960s class was the largest of my seminars. Each Wednesday afternoon, thirty graduate students packed into the narrow wooden rows and enthusiastically played along as I organized a variety of different participatory class exercises. I wanted the course to model the type of education students were demanding at the time. Nevertheless, the homework was fairly traditional -- students digested primary and secondary sources that illuminated various aspects of the era, and they wrote critiques of American culture seen through different lenses.

For the first week of class, I asked students to read a glossy overview of America ca. 1960 – an era in which Jacqueline Kennedy's pillbox hats ruled runways, and many Americans saw the world through the lens of the era's most popular television show about law and order, "Gunsmoke." Thanks to an unprecedented post-war economic boom, the poverty rate in America had dropped to 20%, and the nation's new consumption economy was flourishing, with a television in (almost) every living room and a chicken in (almost) every pot. In class, we looked at photographs and video clips of Kennedy that demonstrated the way he harnessed the power of the media to sway voters.

For the second week of class, we began to dig deeper, and the roots of the 1960s turmoil became more obvious. In 1960, the poverty rate in the U.S. overall was 20%, but it was only 10% for whites as compared with 56% for blacks. There were more ugly numbers: only 20% of African-Americans completed high school, as compared with 43% for whites; and the percentage of black students attending integrated schools in the South in that year was 6.4%. By 1960, the Supreme Court had resolved the case of *Oliver Brown, et al vs. Board of Education of Topeka* (aka *Brown v. Board of Ed*) with a series of five epic rulings, asserting that segregation in public schools was unconstitutional, and that desegregation had to proceed "with all deliberate speed."

Reaction to *Brown v. Board of Ed* in the South

revealed deep and old fault lines. Non-violent civil rights activists who supported the end of segregation were met by those who viciously disagreed, and used police dogs, water cannons, beatings, bombings, and mass incarceration to try and maintain the status quo. Throughout these terrible clashes, the new medium of television was in a majority of living rooms across the country, projecting the hatred and brutality of local officials on a daily basis for all to see. In April 1963, this situation became even more impossible to ignore when Martin Luther King, Jr. was arrested while leading a march in Birmingham, Alabama.

King already was an iconic figure in the movement, due to his brilliant oratory and fierce determination to lead social change as a Baptist minister and civil rights activist. Many religious leaders had joined his cause and marched with King arm-in-arm. However, on April 12, 1963, eight white Alabama clergymen issued a statement urging the protestors in the streets to go home. They were upset that "outsiders" were leading "actions as incite to hatred and violence," that "have not contributed to the resolution of our local problems."

King was far from willing to abandon the cause in Alabama, and so, while still in jail, he drafted an extraordinary response to the eight clergymen that I assigned my students to read. In "Letter from a Birmingham Jail," King wrote:

> . . . it is wrong to urge an individual to cease his efforts to gain his basic constitutional rights because the quest may precipitate violence. Society must protect the robbed and punish the robber.

And in the end, he made a grand argument about the nation's destiny:

> We will reach the goal of freedom in Birmingham and all over the nation, because the goal of America

is freedom. Abused and scorned though we may be,
our destiny is tied up with America's destiny. Before
the pilgrims landed at Plymouth, we were here.
Before the pen of Jefferson etched the majestic words
of the Declaration of Independence across the pages
of history, we were here. For more than two centuries
our forebears labored in this country without wages;
they made cotton king; they built the homes of their
masters while suffering gross injustice and shameful
humiliation– and yet out of a bottomless vitality they
continued to thrive and develop. If the inexpressible
cruelties of slavery could not stop us, the opposition
we now face will surely fail. We will win our
freedom because the sacred heritage of our nation and
the eternal will of God are embodied in our echoing
demands.

My students were understandably moved to write
passionately about King's text. And although they clearly
were writing about American experience, it was obvious too
that they were influenced by the parallel situations in their
own country. They also saw images of inequality and
repression in their new media, and were faced with tangible
proof that their own government was to blame.

In that light, several students addressed the complaint
that King was an "extremist:"

He was somewhat what he called a creative extremist.
Because he was in possession of penetrating eyes to
see the black's downtrodden status, sensitive ears to
hear the black's groan, a magnanimous heart to lobby
and unite every promising force and acute brain to
foresee and evaluate possible consequences of each
action. Significantly, he was daring enough to take
the leadership and resolutely to gain justice rather
than to wait.

Another student went so far as to assert that breaking an unjust law could be a profoundly patriotic act: "He arouse the conscience of the whole community over the injustice and thus show his highest respect for the American constitutional law which advocates human rights, democracy, equality, love and freedom." Everyone in the class agreed that King was right to ignore the eight clergymen and keep on marching – non-violence was an easy sell.

For the next week's class, I assigned the students to read a much more controversial speech – Malcolm X's "The Ballot or the Bullet." Malcolm X was not nearly as obvious a hero as King. He was born Malcolm Little in 1925 to a father who preached that African-Americans should return to Africa. As a result of his father's outspokenness, the Little family was persecuted by the Ku Klux Klan, and Malcolm's early childhood problems led to a life of crime. He spent the years between 1946 and 1952 in a Boston jail, where he joined the Nation of Islam, and took the name El-Hajj Malik El-Shabazz. At the time, the Nation of Islam preached a message of individual empowerment to African American men, urging them to cast off the chains of the past (symbolized by names deriving from slave-owners). El-Shabazz' charismatic personality and gift for writing led to a rapid rise within the Nation of Islam; from 1953-1964, he served as the organization's chief spokesperson. But the events of 1963 and 1964 were transformative for many people, including Malcolm X.

On August 28th, 1963, just four months after the Birmingham March, more than a quarter-million people marched to Washington to hear Martin Luther King's "I have a Dream" speech from the steps of the Lincoln Memorial. But three weeks after that, white supremacists bombed a Birmingham church on a busy Sunday morning, killing four African American girls, ages 11-14. The bombing sparked riots, and the national outcry spurred President Kennedy to seek sweeping civil rights legislation that would undo all the remaining "Jim Crow" laws that had formed the basis for "lawful" discrimination in Southern states. Kennedy never saw his Civil Rights bill passed – he was gunned down on November 22, 1963. The country was traumatized yet again.

The following year, Malcolm X left the Nation of Islam, and began a speaking tour across the country, during which he delivered his most famous speech, "The Ballot or the Bullet." In his speech, Malcolm argued that the philosophy of non-violence amounted to capitulation:

> . . . Think of the image of someone sitting. An old woman can sit. An old man can sit. A chump can sit. A coward can sit. Anything can sit. For you and I have been *sitting* long enough and it's time for you and I to be doing some *standing*. And some *fighting* to back that up . . . Every nation on the African continent that has gotten its independence brought it about through the philosophy of nationalism. And it will take *black* nationalism to bring about the freedom of twenty-two million Afro-Americans here in this country where we have suffered colonialism for the past four hundred years . . . It'll be the ballot, or it'll be the bullet. It'll be liberty or it'll be death. And if you're not ready to pay that price, don't use the word freedom in your vocabulary.

Although I explained how many people in America found Malcolm X's rhetoric inspiring and empowering, my Chinese students definitely were not convinced. In homework and in class discussions, nobody had anything positive to say about "the bullet." They didn't understand how people could make a nation within another nation, and they didn't seem remotely interested in armed revolt. They thought Malcolm X seemed "crazy."

I knew from talking with my students outside of class that in general they were so cynical about their government that they believed every negative story about corruption, brutality, and repression. They wanted less control from top-down administrators about pretty much everything. However, I can't say I met anyone angry and organized enough to follow someone like Malcolm X out into the street – they mostly wanted to vent. None of them even seemed poised to wear a confrontational tee shirt, let alone pick up a poster and head downtown, or out onto the grounds of the campus.

After I chatted about this class subject with a Chinese friend, she wrote me a long e-mail regarding a conversation she had with a co-worker:

> I simply do not see a realistic future where the Communist Party is overthrown by rebels. I had a conversation with one of my coworkers about this issue.
>
> "What do you think of these rebels going against the Party?" I asked.
>
> "I just don't think they will ever win. The Party is so powerful that fighting with it is almost like suicide."
>
> "Do you sometimes feel that you want to protest in the street like what people do in Hong Kong?"
>
> "Not really. I mean why bother? The economy is going well. It's not like the 60s when everyone was starving. Now I have a good job and a family to care about, so I just want a peaceful life. I don't like protests. They are useless here and will only create more problems."
>
> I think this represents a lot of people's opinions. Martin Luther King fought all the way to

win rights for black people because at that time they were really treated badly and alienated in their own country. But in today's China, on a day-to-day basis I can't say I feel constantly suppressed by the Party, except sometimes annoyed by censorship. The government can still make good policies from time to time that benefit the people, like infrastructure and transportation. The more prosperous China becomes, the more grateful the people will be; this is what the Party thinks. This is definitely false, but I do think that as long as people are content with their jobs and money, they won't really care enough about politics to revolt.

When I looked around my classroom and thought about the students and colleagues I knew well, this assessment seemed pretty accurate. The situation would have to get much more dire for Chinese academics and students before they would be radicalized enough to face down police in the streets. On the other hand, it also is unlikely that the government can keep up the flow of "jobs and money" indefinitely. Without a foundation of trust, the government can't expect much support if (and when) the bubble bursts. And avoiding that grim possibility would require a huge amount of change. But can the CPC change as it is presently constituted?

On their final exams, I asked my students to discuss "what they had learned from America in the 1960s about how change can take place in a large, diverse, and complex nation." The answers were insightful. Some students commented that the most important requirement for change was that it had to come both from the top and bottom of society – both through 'powerful' leadership and 'common awakening:'

Change requires: 1. "The consciousness and awakening of different kinds of people, who feel disappointed with their situation and feel it necessary to change it. 2. A powerful leader and advanced ideology which can unite them together to fight . . . 3. A clear objective and real efforts to realize it.

Another student agreed, using one the many idioms Chinese students learning English are forced to memorize: "More hands make light work." This was an obvious but important point: protest can't work unless a huge number of people turn out over and over again, as we saw in watching videos of Montgomery, Birmingham, Washington, D.C., etc. There are an abundance of "more hands" in China, but the "powerful leader" piece is much more uncertain.

The answers got more interesting, and more directly applicable to the Chinese situation, when students delved more deeply into specifics. Several commented on American economics in the 1960s, for example:

> In the economic booming, there still were large numbers of people living in poverty, the condition of whom was even worse because the fast development had widened the income gap. Therefore, they also wanted a trend of transformation.

Another student gave this point of view an even more Chinese slant:

> From the Marxism point of view, "economic basis determines the superstructure," which means all changes must begin with the change of economy. After the WWII, America became an affluent society. The wealth, on one hand enlarged the economic gap between the black and white, the poor and rich. The tension between these groups became more obvious. On the other hand, the wealth ensured that more people can have a higher education. The students have more time and leisure time. They're educated, thus can think critically.

If we replace 'America after WWII,' with 'China after Reform and Opening,' this would be an eerily close description of the contemporary situation. Another similarity was striking in a student's answer as well:

> With the development of technology, communication is easier than before. Machines saved many time for people to work. So they have more free time to get together talking discussing about the social problems showed by the media. With the help of technology, they could even communicate with people far from each other. And this communicate methods bond them together to fight for what they wanted to have. With the development of technology, people does and could come together for change.

Technically, none of these students was actually writing about China. But they were writing about America through China-colored glasses, and what they were describing is all the change that is happening right now – a convergence of growing education, economic interest, communication, leisure, and critical thinking. At a certain point, these students might just experience a "common awakening" if they felt that the cause had an ethical and "clear objective" -- just as most Americans who protested in 1963 probably could not have imagined doing so in 1960. As one observant student wrote, the change would not have to arise from the masses at the outset:

> Looking back, one may find all these changes occurring spontaneously in a certain place, targeting initially at the local level, and gradually spreading its influence to the whole country.

Another student agreed:

> Social political and economic systems are intertwined with each other. The whole society is established like a domino, if one area is knock down, then others will

follow and an inevitable change would take place. If there is a first domino to fall in China, it's unlikely to be in wealthy, relatively liberal Guangzhou. There are, of course, plenty of other candidates, across the country.

A Visit to Xinjiang

The most interesting lecture invitation I received arrived in my e-mail inbox in January. I needn't have been especially flattered, since Xinjiang Normal University was one of a handful of institutions with a diligent foreign expert administrator who invited every single Fulbrighter. Nevertheless, I was pretty excited about the trip. Xinjiang province is about the farthest and most exotic destination on the circuit. In May, after a five-hour flight, I arrived at the big new airport in Urumqi, and was met by a professor and graduate student with somewhat limited English. We drove on a big, new highway into the city, and then on to the campus of the University, which had invited me to give two lectures on American art and culture. Although my campus visit was similar in many ways to others I already had completed, visiting Xinjiang definitely was different. This trip led me to view China's political future in a much harsher light.

The flight to Urumqi took so long because Xinjiang is really far from Guangzhou. It juts out into Europe, rising above Tibet and India. Its western border abuts Kazakhstan, Kyrgyzstan, Tajikistan, Afghanistan, and Pakistan; to the North is Russia, and to the East are the relatively poor and unsettled provinces of Qinghai and Gansu. Any place that borders so many troubled regions is likely to be a hotspot, but the particular historical development of Xinjiang all but guarantees unrest. The region changed hands many times before 1949, existing sometimes as part of China, and sometimes as a struggling independent state called East Turkmenistan Republic, established by the predominant Muslim Uyghur ethnic group.

Mao was not interested in permitting a Muslim Republic in what he considered to be Han Chinese land, so in 1949, the CPC sent troops to bring what they considered their natural territory back into the fold. A mass migration of Han into the region followed (some willing and some not), and today the region has about forty percent Uyghur, and forty-five percent Han people, plus forty-odd other distinct cultural and linguistic groups, spread out across a sparsely-populated region that makes up one-sixth of China's total territory. We had considered taking a long family trip to visit various exotic ancient Silk Road cities in Xinjiang, but after reading about the annual outbursts of violent attacks by separatist groups, we decided on a different destination, and I went to Urumqi just for four days, on my own.

My first lecture went extremely well. About two hundred students from the art school showed up to hear about Modern American Art, which kept the students awake. Google translator came up with the following English version of the review posted on the campus website the next day:

> The contents of the report, focused, rigorous logic, the majority of teachers and students inspired. During his speech, Amy Werbel Professor cited on behalf of the people and representative works of each period, also actively interact with the students, the atmosphere is extremely active. . . The Werbel Professor of you teachers and students, their questions, 11 answers seriously, won rounds of applause of the scene of teachers and students.

The fuss made about my visit was amusing and sweet – there were lots of introductions and exchanges of business cards and gifts, attention from the President of the University, and a welcome party at which I impressed my hosts by drinking the same *baijiu* as the men (albeit in much smaller quantities). Some of my Fulbright friends who visited before me even had billboards made with their pictures.

Urumqi didn't strike me as much different than other places I had visited in China until that night, when I went online using the computer set up in my hotel room. Every time I tried to get some information about Urumqi and Xinjiang, I was redirected to a government website. The television was even more heavily propagandistic, broadcasting 18 channels of CCTV (the government media organization), followed by 8 channels of Xinjiang TV, all playing nonstop, ludicrous propaganda.

There were soap operas about Revolutionary-era Communist generals fighting evil, which are popular all over the Mainland, and local Han police fighting evil. What really mesmerized me, though, were the channels of Uyghur dancing, hosted by Han Chinese men extolling the virtues and beauties of the Motherland, interspersed with "Little Miss Xinjiang"-style displays of tiny kids performing graceful dance moves in traditional costumes. The camera cut back and forth to an audience of weepy people in the audience watching the "pageant" of ethnic minorities, singing and dancing in traditional costumes, all in the name of extolling their allegiance to the Motherland.

On a tour of the Provincial Museum the next day, I was amazed by the level of propaganda built into the display of this complicated territory. At the entrance to the first gallery, a sign read:

> We have selected a batch of fine works and run this exhibition of these precious relics and auxiliary exhibits from the Stone Age to Qing Dynasty for the purpose to show the contributions the people of all nationalities in Xinjiang have made for safeguarding

of the reunification of the motherland, for enriching
the motherland's cultural treasure-house, and to make
the masses of audience receive the education in
patriotism.

Despite the fascinating displays, the Uyghur people I met
didn't seem as though they had absorbed the "education in
patriotism." And undoubtedly, the separatists who killed
hundreds of Han Chinese in the streets of Urumqi just two
years earlier also didn't get the message about being happy to
"reunify."

On the weekend, a young professor, her boyfriend,
and a graduate student accompanied me on a trip to the
lovely oasis town of Turpan, which is famous for producing
dried fruits. They all identified themselves as Han Chinese.
The professor, from Nanjing, hated living there, but it was a
good job, and employment as an art professor was not an
easy thing. She seemed to be working on interesting projects
with her students, judging from the work in the campus
gallery. The two men in the car, on the other hand, were
third-generation Xinjiang residents. The student's
grandfather had emigrated in the 1950s, during "The Great
Leap Forward" when the PRC was encouraging Han
settlement of Western territories as a means of securing the
region. The boyfriend's grandfather had been stationed in
Urumqi as a soldier at that time, and likewise had been
"strongly encouraged" to stay when he was decommissioned.

During the two-hour drive out of town, we saw the
largest wind farm in China – a massive project clearly sited
in the perfect spot. We also passed gas wells, and the
construction sites for a pipeline that will carry Xinjiang's
prodigious supply of natural gas east – to Shanghai. Two
more pipelines are planned, which also will bring energy
from Xinjiang to eastern areas of China. The dry, blazing hot
land was a rich red hue. Sporadically, we could see low

rectangular buildings that held entrances to earth-bermed houses popular in nearby regions including Afghanistan. This was, after all, an area well-traveled by Silk Road traders. But the small red historical remains were dwarfed by the enormous energy production facilities.

I asked the boyfriend, a petrochemical engineer trained in Beijing and Singapore, if there was much discussion at his workplace about environmental issues. He actually seemed amused by the question, and replied without hesitation: "No. Never." Looking out the window of the car, that assessment seemed right on target. I diplomatically praised the amazing investment the government had made in the region, and then asked my companions whether it seemed like the development money was helping ease some of the tensions with the Uyghur people. The response was not encouraging: "We don't know what they want– we don't talk to them." They also told me that they didn't know any words in Uyghur.

When I asked whether Uyghurs worked in the oil and gas fields the boyfriend replied: "No, they wouldn't like that kind of job – the living conditions are too harsh. They get migrant workers from Sichuan and other mainland provinces. The Uyghur people just make the fruit, and do the tourism." My Han car buddies, on the other hand, were thrilled about the investment, especially the boyfriend: "There's a lot of money here." At one point in my delicate probing about Uyghur relations, the student turned to me and said sharply: "I'm a local too." There aren't many easy conversations in Xinjiang.

When planning my visit beforehand, the foreign expert administrator asked what I wanted to do during my visit, and I naively replied that I wanted to eat as much Uyghur food as possible, and shop in a Uyghur market. I wanted the "authentic" Xinjiang experience, and the local specialties sounded fantastic – grilled lamb, rice pilao, and puffed bread. I was definitely ready for a break from Chinese food. My naïve request, however, turned out to be unexpectedly problematic. It took a really long time to find a restaurant for lunch, because we kept getting turned away, reportedly because the staff would not agree to give my hosts a receipt for reimbursement. I asked whether it would be comfortable to live in Turpan as a Han Chinese. The dry answer came quickly from one of the students, "At a certain point, no." He then told me that he never ate Uyghur food. This was definitely not turning out to be my most diplomatic trip in China.

Nonetheless, when we finally did find a restaurant that would serve us, it was impossible to think about politics while eating the delicious, heaping platters of lamb, rice, and stuffed vegetables. The grilled bread was charred and crispy, and the eggplant dip was creamy and garlicky. The flavors and textures reminded me of Middle Eastern food, having pretty much nothing in common with the "Chinese" dishes I was used to. As we finished lunch, the room next door came to life with a party of Uyghur men, playing traditional instruments, dancing, and smoking hookahs. When they saw me listening near the door, they invited me in to dance with them, and I did. Everyone was laughing, even my Han companions.

The next day, I met a new group of hosts in the morning, and we headed off for a day at the Uyghur market in Urumqi. The delicate woman from Nanjing who had been willing to go to Turpan had a sudden "emergency" and bowed out. In her place, she sent a Han graduate student who spoke some English, the Uyghur secretary from the department and her sister, an English teacher at a local bilingual high school. The Uyghur women were extremely beautiful, with broad faces, cheerful smiles, and frilly clothing. The younger sister wore the long braid traditional for Uyghur women, while her older sister chose a shorter style, with a chignon at the nape of her neck. Both of them wore striking makeup, with dark eyeliner, and big, matching sets of gold earrings, bracelets, and rings.

My entourage was a bit awkward, to say the least. With one Han, and two Uyghur guides, I sometimes felt as though I had been called in to settle a diplomatic schism between warring enemies. The tension was not subtle. For one thing, following my request, we headed straight for Urumqi's "other side of the tracks," and it was pretty clear that this made the Han man very nervous. He told me that the city is strictly divided, with the Han majority living in more upscale neighborhoods on the other side of the highway. Much of the Uyghur neighborhood we walked through was in the process of being torn down to make way for new construction. Although SUVs with soldiers bearing semi-automatic rifles were visible, they clearly didn't make my Han host feel more comfortable.

I should have been more empathetic than I was. When asking in Guangzhou whether I should be worried about traveling in Uyghur areas, I repeatedly was told: "only if you're Han, they wouldn't bother a Westerner." The ultimate white privilege is not being gunned down or stabbed because of your genetics. Nevertheless, nothing bad happened and the Uyghur market was a delight. Amidst the lace covers for washing machines, toilet bowls, and tissue boxes, the frilly carriers for potluck dishes, and the gaudy gold jewelry, I found beautiful textiles, including well-made woven and embroidered wool scarves, and covers for couches and pillows. I also bought a lot of dried fruits to give as gifts in Guangzhou. The Uyghur women stuck close, leaving the Han man to walk behind, staring nervously at his watch.

Time was an interesting indication of how bad relations are in Xinjiang. I had to catch a plane at six, but when I asked the time, the Han man said four, while the younger Uyghur woman said two – she proudly showed me that she sets her watch to what should be the correct local time, not Beijing time as enforced by the CPC throughout China. She admitted that this caused a lot of confusion in the province: "People always have to ask which time are you using when they make a meeting." The plane, of course, was on CPC and not East Turkmenistan time, so we had to go.

I asked another tricky question over lunch as well. Where do Uyghur people come from originally? The Han man quickly answered: "from Mongolia." "Really?" the young Uyghur woman barked back at him. She looked at me fiercely. "Do I look Mongolian?" "No," I said, "you kind of remind me of my Romanian grandmother." She was triumphant. "Yes, of course, we are European! From Eastern Europe!" The Han man just rolled his eyes. Later, online, I read about many more contentious battles over the historical record that have inflamed Uyghur anger.

Daily irritations and religious differences are layered on top of historical animosity in Xinjiang, and together these all form a pretty toxic brew. The young teacher told me that that even though the school she teaches at is technically bilingual, the students learn everything in Mandarin, except for her class in reading and writing in Uyghur, which meets just a few hours a week. She is responsible for three classes of students, each with close to sixty students. Still, she told me, the school is fairly liberal, because if other teachers occasionally speak to students in Uyghur, they didn't get punished. In Kashgar, a much more heavily Uyghur and much poorer city further south, she said that a teacher would get fired for doing that, and that the headmaster constantly watches them. She seemed happy to live in Urumqi instead, which is much more lively and fun, although she added that it is getting too expensive.

Despite the worries of my Han companions, the end of my weekend went off without a hitch. They seemed relieved to drop me at the airport, my luggage now stuffed with Uyghur textiles and fruits. The security at the airport was much greater than any I had experienced in China, with lots of bomb-sniffing dogs, hand swabs, and two rounds of x-ray screening. As it turns out, the extra security was well-advised. A few weeks later, newspapers reported an attempted plane hijacking by Xinjiang terrorists. According to the *China Daily News*, several passengers, including a Uyghur police officer, wrestled the hijackers to the ground and the flight was saved. The reporter concluded that: "The success in foiling this attempted hijacking means that maintaining the stability and prosperity of Xinjiang has become a common goal for people from all ethnic groups." I doubt my new Uyghur friends read the episode quite in that way. Once again, the parallel universe created by Chinese control of the media only puts a happy face on things – it doesn't change the reality. Xinjiang is not okay, and the Uyghur people are unlikely to become fans of the "motherland" any time soon.

The Question of Social and Political Change

If China does have a domino-like wave of change, it won't be pretty. In our history, protests, bullets, and ballots all at one point or another have resulted in government that more closely reflected the will of the governed. Our Constitution is a great keel to have in the throes of stormy seas, and both Martin and Malcolm were able to draw on a rich precedent of American legislators and freedom fighters in making their case. As one insightful student wrote:

The turbulent sixties didn't come without a historical tradition. As early as the founding of the United States, the Constitution had already define "life, liberty, and the pursuit of happiness" as "inalienable rights" for its citizens. . . The American Dream promises freedom with prosperity and fullest development of one's own. The spirit of freedom and individualism has long become the national ethos of America. Without this spirit, changes would not take place in such an enormous way.

For another student, our "liberal political system" was key:

A liberal political system is essential to guarantee the implementation of social changes. In an autocratic political system, it is hard for protestor's voices to be heard due to suppression. Even if protestors made to convey their appeals to public opinions, the autocratic government may be reluctant to make change if it may affect its interests.

And for a third student, our diversity made it possible for new ideas to spur change:

America is a large, diverse, and complex nation, and American society is considered as a melting pot of diverse cultures. So, in one sense, the open and welcome American diverse culture laid a foundation for the existence of other conflicting cultures and beliefs.

The contrast with China was implicit in all these comments. My students all were well aware that the rhetoric of their government and culture didn't support "freedom," "individualism," pluralistic politics, or the notion of "diversity." Even though the social conditions in China are similar in many ways to 1960 in America, the same prerequisites for radical change within one government simply aren't there.

As I was preparing to come back to the United States, I asked my Chinese students and colleagues if they were keeping an eye on the upcoming party "elections" in Beijing, slated for the following fall. The potential embedded in this change of leadership was big news in Hong Kong and New York, but the people I asked all said no -- what was the point? The decisions would be made "behind closed doors," and at some point they could watch the transfer ceremony on television.

Americans certainly are blessed in that regard. We still have at least the bones of a remarkably flexible and sturdy system of government. When our side loses, we can start thinking about the next election, and how we can promote our viewpoint on the way there. In every election cycle, we have the chance to to participate, and then to watch the tangible outcome when the reins of power are peacefully transferred -- granted by the "consent of the governed." This democratic scenario isn't coming to Beijing anytime soon.

Ultimately, the question of social and political change in China may be as much about technology and economics as it is about politics. At some point, CPC censors may not be able to prevent the Malcolm X – or the Ai Wei Wei – from becoming a powerful leader. They may not be able to provide the jobs and goods that give people hope and satisfaction. Environmental problems, already staggering in their scale, will only increase. If real electoral change is not a possibility, that doesn't leave a lot of options.

Whatever happens, China's playbook and destiny will be entirely its own; after teaching this unit, I came to think that our 1960s isn't a great guide. China must and will change, but not because there is some inevitable, global, historical arc bending towards justice. The people I met in China generally had good prospects (at the moment), and could look back on decades of overall progress (even if there were lots of problems with that). But nobody should think that this situation is terribly stable. The dominos are stacked close together, and the end pieces in the lineup – in places like Xinjiang and Wukan -- are wobbling precariously. The CPC doesn't have an inspiring narrative that young people are invested in, or care to watch on television, and it doesn't have a mechanism for peaceful social change if "mass incidents" exceed their capacity to maintain control. I hope for the sake of all my students, colleagues, and friends that the CPC will go back to the path of reform and opening that has allowed the country to prosper, and that will permit China to write a truly new chapter in its history.

Chapter Seven. China's Reform and Opening Generation vs. Hippies

When we first arrived in Guangzhou during the incredibly hot month of August, I noticed that Chinese women chose much higher necklines than many of my American students, who tended to let it all hang out. At home, you could tell the seasons by how much chest was on display, and come May, the situation got ridiculous. To put it bluntly, there was a lot less cleavage, and cleavage-gawking on the streets of China. However, it wasn't exactly as if everyone was modest. Instead of America's low necklines and Victoria's Secret-hoisted bosoms, female Chinese students favored booty shorts, by which I mean shorts so short they really should count as underwear. In winter, students often wore them over dreadfully clashing tights, in neon colors, or harlequin checkers. Add to that a pair of 4-inch high platform heels and you had what Anna Wintour definitely would declare a national fashion disaster.

But it gets even more strange than that, because next to the booty-short, tight and heel perpetrator, there usually was a young woman dressed as though she was headed for a bar mitzvah in New York, ca. 1970 – layers and layers of pale chiffon and dainty heels (often with nylon peds), in the middle of the week, in a college classroom. And next to her, the most ubiquitous of all, the girl wearing jeans and a tee shirt sporting a mash-up of slightly-off American trademark logos, mixed with Jabberwockian English slogans: Girls is the Powers! Wean from the Mighty Force! Love, Meanings, Express! Georgeo Amrani! The boys wore the Jabberwockian shirts as well, typically rumpled and hanging outside of baggy jeans.

The credit (or blame) for China's fashion diversity today can be fairly assigned to Deng Xiaoping, who first launched China's "Reform and Opening" movement in 1979. Before Deng, the drab "Mao suit" was required and ubiquitous. But after defeating Maoist hard-liners to seize power, Deng opened doors to the West for trade, investment, cultural exchanges – and bad tee shirts. He established innovative and experimental Special Economic Zones to spur growth; and allowed capitalist reforms of many state-owned enterprises. The economic growth that resulted was miraculous. When the Chinese people once again were permitted to profit from their own hard work and entrepreneurial skills, they did so – in spades. And the government prospered in even more spades.

Today's college students were born a decade into Deng's miraculous era of transformation. By the time my Chinese students were headed off to middle school, even tottering elderly people were walking down urban Chinese streets talking in ancient dialects on cell phones, and most young people in cities spent a lot of time on the Internet – watching videos on Youkou (Chinese Youtube), keeping in touch with their friends on QQ (primarily an instant messaging service), playing games, and reading lots of microblogs and Twitter-like feeds called Weibo. Today, more than 510 million Chinese use the Internet – almost double the entire population of the United States.

In the West, all of this is seen as a wonderful miracle, one made even better by the fact that urban Chinese kids adore American brands like KFC, Pizza Hut, Coke, Apple, and Nike. Whatever criticism we may have of the Chinese government, there is no quibbling with the fact that they have enabled today's college students to grow up during a period of extraordinary economic expansion. The generation that comes closest is that of the American "baby boomers" in the mid-20th century. This historical parallel made me think it would be especially significant, and fun, to see how my students would respond to the legendarily "unharmonious" behaviors of our own American "Reform and Opening" baby boom generation.

In November, we began our discussion of the 1960s counter-culture in America by studying the Free Speech Movement (FSM) that caused a series of disruptions at the University of California, Berkeley in 1964 and 1965. For their homework, I assigned the students to read part of an anthology called the *Portable Sixties Reader* containing speech excerpts and song lyrics by FSM participants, including Dave Mandel, Lee Felsenstein, Richard Kampf, Dan Paik, and Richard Schmorleitz. Along with Mario Savio and Jack Weinberg, they were among the many UC Berkeley undergraduates who were involved in protesting the House Un-American Activities Committee hearings in Washington. A number of them had also gone to Mississippi to register black voters during "Freedom Summer." When they got back to campus in 1963 and 1964, they agitated to get local businesses to hire black employees, and protested against ultra-conservative politicians. On campus, they set up shop to distribute leaflets and raise awareness of the Civil Rights movement and free speech issues at the University.

The Regents of the University of California were not happy about the students' activities. Conservative politicians and local business owners put pressure on them to clamp things down, and the Regents responded by banning pamphleteering and other forms of advocacy on or adjacent to the campus. When five students were brought up on disciplinary charges for breaking the new rules, five hundred showed up for punishment. The next month, when Jack Weinberg was arrested for flouting the ban, Mario Savio famously stood atop the police car in which Weinberg and his police escort were sitting. Savio and others proceeded to make speeches for thirty-two straight hours, standing on top of the immobilized car.

The next month, when more than one thousand students took over the chief Administration building, Sproul Hall, nearly eight hundred of them were taken to jail. Soon after, the faculty rallied to their aid, and the Academic Senate ruled that the students should have free speech rights on campus. Rather than riling a vast majority of the faculty, the Regents quickly made peace by replacing the conservative Chancellor, Edward Strong, with the more liberal Martin Meyerson, and from then on Berkeley was the site of near constant (but legal) protests. Then-Governor Ronald Reagan was incensed, but free speech had prevailed.

To raise money for their cause, the students wrote and published a small songbook in early 1964, which formed part of the homework my students had to read for class. The introduction to the songbook recommended: "Sing them loud and sing them often. You will be helping to fight the battle for Constitutional rights." The songs included these stanzas by Lee Felsenstein:

> I'm going to put my name down, brother, where do I sign?
> Sometimes you have to lay your body on the line,
> We're going to make this campus free
> And keep it safe for democracy.

And, by Dan Paik:

> I read my Constitution long ago
> I read the Bill of Rights, read it nice and slow
> I don't know much but this I know
> They ain't got no right to take my name.

Mario Savio's willingness to risk his body and life atop a squad car for the cause had generated enormous support for the movement. His example led many Berkeley students to vow to stand together: If one student was singled out, many more would band together, making campus "discipline" practically impossible to restore.

This generational bond reminded me very much of my Chinese students, who spent all their time together attending the same classes as other majors in their fields, and living together in crowded dorm rooms. Strolling across the green and lush campus, it was common to see female friends walking hand-in-hand or arm-in-arm, and male friends seemed more physically chummy than in America as well. One young woman explained that the strong friendships among her generation were in part driven by the one-child policy. Most of them were only children, and so they called their friends "sister" or "brother" in an attempt to make up for their feelings of loneliness.

I fully expected that Savio, et al., would not impress all of my Chinese students; the Berkeley students' behavior was way out-of-keeping with expectations in China of respect for elders and authority figures. However, to my surprise, only a small minority thought the students had gone too far. On the negative side, one student wrote:

> Young people tend to get irrational when they find the satisfaction of being "someone", as a student leader one could become a "press secretary" who have to "find time from his duty" to write just a song. And this sense of heroism could most easily and most often achieved in confrontational effort against the government. They turn this protest for peace into a war: a war against government, police, school board, and even "anyone over thirty". Social protest finally became their "show of might". It eventually evolved into a counter culture movement in which the shapes of peace and ideal are barely recognizable. But here a question remains: is it right to "let young people think

they have the right to choose the laws they would obey as long as they were doing it in the name of social protest"?

Another student didn't question the students' law-breaking, but thought that they had acted in an immature and self-defeating way:

It is, of course, imperative for them to take some actions to raise the issue. However, as they formed the main force in conducting the campaigns, their adolescent arrogance and imprudence, specially embodied in some extreme action, stirred more unrest than approval from the society. Represented by the immature students, the movements might be labeled, in some Americans' eyes, as radical and extreme. Thus the public might be even more hostile to the protests than to the issues they brought about.

Although it certainly is true that sit-ins, strikes, etc., did alienate some Americans from the free speech cause, in contrast to these two students, the vast majority of the class thought the students' actions were entirely defensible. Response to the FSM was about 21 for, and just 4 against.

As to the justice of the cause, several students rightly noted that the FSM was a natural outgrowth of the Civil Rights movement: "The students shared similar goals with the civil rights activists, aiming to fight for citizen's rights, freedom of speech and political action by peaceful means." FSM was able to further the cause, because it:

. . . makes people rethink the laws and values advocated by the government, and begin to question the authority and the older generation. . . What is right and wrong is no longer decided by the propaganda of the government or the press. Second, FSM makes people confident in their ability to change what they feel wrong. People are encouraged to fight for their democracy and freedom. Just as showed in the lyrics, they believe they should shout to "wake up" all the people, and believe their fight will lead to a promising "morning". . . The government can repress an individual, but can never defeat the overwhelming majority. . . word of mouth, and thus it cannot be repressed by the authority.

Another young woman also wrote about the power of music: "Because the fire could be quelled down, the innocent students could be put in jail, but the voice, the united voice could never be suppressed by any violence in any form."

One young woman noted that it was right for the students to agitate because they have the "strongest power to fight with the administration:"

First and for most, they have ideology weapon and methodology. The higher education equips the university students with the advanced ideology of freedom, democracy, equality to discern what is right and what is wrong as well as methodology of how to put minds into reality. Secondly, university is the place where lives the best capable people, leaders, elites, lecturers who can advocate and lead people to fight with any power they target at. Thirdly, the campus facilities can be made the most of to "plan, organize, implement, raise fund, recruit participants" for anti-administration actions. Fourthly, so solid and integrated is the community that it would not be easily frightened away into individuals. From the beginning they form a group, it would be a community which would suffer no individual to be singled out for punishment for what all have done or should have done. They would never abandon one another until the problem is solved. One more thing to add, though less important, the university students have nothing to lose, economically or socially

whether or not they win or lose in the combat.

This was a complex answer that encapsulated almost all the arguments made by the other students over and over again.

The student's first point, that University students have advanced "ideology of freedom, democracy, equality to discern what is right and what is wrong as well as methodology of how to put minds into reality" struck me as an extremely idealistic portrayal of the education at American universities. We hadn't discussed the American education system very much, but I realized when reading this how much I emphasized over the course of the semester that I considered this to be an "American" classroom in the south of China.

It certainly was very different than their Chinese courses, with far less lecturing, and far more open discussion of controversial topics. They had to comment on the reading for every class in their required homework assignments, instead of being graded principally on huge exams requiring memorization. They could like it or hate it, I told them, but I would give them a taste of what it felt like to be a student in my American classroom. One student wrote that: "Universities and colleges should be places where the wind of freedom blows," but it was interesting to me (and disheartening) that she wrote that while sitting in an institution where there is only the slightest hint of a breeze.

I thought about academic freedom a great deal during my year in China. Although I was given exceptional latitude as a visiting Fulbright scholar to "do what ever I wanted," the students and faculty were far from "free." The whole concept of academic freedom in fact gained a new dimension for me over the course of the year, but especially during my very last week on campus.

In the spring term, a new Dean was appointed, and

she asked me to help advise the administrators of the English Department, including Vice Deans and Party Secretaries, on a problem they were having. The operative five-year plan for GDUFS included ambitious new goals for hiring more foreign professors, sending more students abroad, and even attracting foreign students. But the different credit model of the American and Chinese Universities was making it hard to transfer credits. The Dean kindly sent me their undergraduate course requirement list to analyze, so that I could prepare a presentation comparing the American and Chinese curricula. The document was a lengthy, mad laundry list of dozens of required courses, with little opportunity to choose elective courses based on interest.

Even among the elective courses, all of the offerings were broad and generic; a typical example was a course entitled "British Poetry." In a typical American liberal arts program, the differences are enormous. Students typically fulfill "core" requirements by choosing among many options. Chinese students in contrast are assigned to majors before they even arrive on campus, and then given a long and specific list of courses to take, marching arm-in-arm with their classmates through three and a half years, until they are expected to go off to internships in the spring of their senior year.

Despite the enormous differences in the two systems, I ultimately thought the credit-transfer problem wouldn't be difficult to fix at all. GDUFS students take plenty of credits per semester, except that theirs are almost all in two-credit courses, while American courses typically each have three or four credits. I suggested in our administrative meeting that if they simply bundled pairs of courses together, their student's transcripts would have transferrable credits in the American system. For example, they could put the separate courses "Translation" and "Interpretation" together into one course.

Two different faculty members still could teach the subjects, as long as they could agree on one course number and title, and one final grade.

The Deans and Party Secretaries looked at me with relatively blank stares, and I asked if they thought that would be possible. "We can't do that," the Dean replied. "We can't make those changes." "Well," I asked, "who makes those decisions? How do you change your curriculum?" They laughed. They don't make the curriculum – they *receive* the curriculum from the CPC Ministry of Education – including the course requirements for the majors, and even the textbooks used for the courses, which are prepared and approved by committees. The resulting education bears very few similarities to the way my students in America learn, or the way American faculty govern their classrooms and institutions (in the best case scenarios) . . . just a glimmer of a breeze of freedom, indeed. They were free to listen to my presentation and ask lots of questions about how we do things in America, but they weren't actually free to do anything about it. Chinese faculty members are more than just ham-strung; they are fundamentally disempowered. At Berkeley, the faculty had a huge role to play in supporting student protestors. In a Chinese university, that would be impossible.

Given the contrast in the respective educational systems, it is not surprising that many of my Chinese students seemed particularly passionate about the ideals of higher education in the American model, and seemed quite angry by the idea that the U.C. Berkeley administration would interfere with that sacred mission:

> As the head of the administration, the chancellor might hold a view that the students come to the campus, where they should conform to the regularities, to study as the priority for they were still

immature "children". The chancellor and regents would act like "nannies" who gingerly followed their children for fear that they would touch the sphere of politics which might bring the university in awkward situation. On the contrary, the college students, though without social experience, composed the fresh blood of a country. They got access to latest academic reports and were all the time trained to think reflectively and to speak out their thoughts. Since there was the Bill of Rights to guarantee the citizen's freedom of speech, their meetings and forums to discuss about the political activities in the campus were justified and reasonable. Moreover, the Civil Rights Movement and anti-Vietnam War demonstrations aroused their attention to country affairs. All these factors induced their protests. The chancellor could listen to what the students were trying to speak even though there were disapprovals from other trustees and government. Their speech might not be that naïve, erroneous and derailed from what they had learnt in the campus.

Echoing the sentiments of the American baby boom generation, this was a fairly clear statement that young people, the "fresh blood of a country," are more than just children. Their opinions matter and can even be more correct than their elders.

Another student took a similar view, and thought that the Regents had made a mistake to ever try and curtail free speech rights on campus:

This group of students was like a pot of boiling water. President Clark Kerr's decision was like a gesture to seal the boiling pot. It's dangerous to stop the way as outlet of the students' strong emotion. Their reaction could be out of control as a result. It would be wiser

for President Clark Kerr to find some milder way to
lead students to express their passion in a better
manner. Probably, he might launch a debate about the
student's concern in local newspaper, or hold
speeches to show the complexity of the current affairs
to students.

A third student described the rise of the FSM in broad terms
that could be applied equally to his own generation:

At that time, American people have achieved a lot in
their material life, they begin to feel indignant of the
repressive cultural environment. So the citizens,
especially those students who are young and
aggressive, try to release their resentment through
initiating the FSM. This is a manifestation of their
desire for freedom, equality and peace, which are
essential elements of a smooth and stable society.

In keeping with the theme of free speech, we spent the whole
eighty-minute session the next week conducting debates on
propositions such as: "The student actions at U.C. Berkeley
were justified" and "What is the line between rightful protest
and violent criminality?" The students loved the debate
format of class so much that I scheduled several more in the
weeks to come.

Like teaching Martin Luther King, Jr., I thought FSM
was pretty tame stuff. After all, the American college
students were campaigning for justice and liberty, and used
peaceful, non-violent means (such as writing cute songs) to
achieve their goals. I wondered how they would respond to
other aspects of 1960s youth counter-culture.

In America, my students often romanticize the hippies
of the 1960s, especially since they still admire the music. But
Chinese students' view of "counter-culture" is far more
complex, insofar as it challenges still-revered family
hierarchies, notions of success, and the possibilities they

imagine for choosing their own paths. Even just on the face of things American hippies and Chinese Reform and Opening kids look like they have nothing in common. I asked my son Graham why so many students (even English majors) wore those tee shirts with meaningless incorrect slogans and he said that Chinese students liked the meaninglessness. If they wore a shirt with a slogan in Chinese, it might be misinterpreted. As Graham explained, "Every Chinese character is filled with thousands of years of changing and multiplying connotations and people fear that with wearing a witty Chinese slogan, they might be judged." With English gibberish, nobody bothers to read the shirts. The clothing, as a result, is entirely apolitical. The students' politics (if they have any) are their own business. My Chinese students simply were not that interested in actively "countering" or protesting anything. This became especially clear when we talked about one of the cornerstones of hippie anti-authoritarian experience: hallucinogenic drugs.

At the same time Chinese people were suffering the horrible atrocities of their Cultural Revolution, another cultural revolution was taking place on the other side of the globe. One of its chief instigators was Timothy Leary, a psychology professor at Harvard University who began experimenting with hallucinogenic psilocybin mushrooms and later their synthesized equivalent, LSD, in 1960. For homework, my students read his essay "Turning on the World," a vivid depiction of a weekend of tripping at his house with Allen Ginsberg, "secretary-general of the world's poets, beatniks, anarchists, socialists, free-sex/love cultists," other poets, and a couple of Harvard students. He was fired from his position soon after, in 1963.

Leary was born in 1920, and rose to academic prominence through his research on the therapeutic potential of LSD and psilocybin mushrooms for treating psychological disorders such as alcoholism, as well as the use of psilocybin in traditional indigenous Mexican communities for religious purposes. He wasn't the only person experimenting with LSD and mushrooms at the time (the drugs were still legal until 1966), but he was the first to loudly advocate that they be used for spiritual purposes in the general public. Over the course of the decade following his "liberation" from Harvard, Leary advocated that young people: "turn on, tune in, and drop out," which became a rallying-cry for many in the counter-culture movement.

"Turning on the World" describes a weekend at Leary's house just before his expulsion from Harvard. While Allen Ginsberg and two other poets are wandering in and out of the house tripping, sometimes naked, sometimes vomiting, Leary's son, daughter, and teenage friends are coming and going, essentially left to fend for themselves. At the height of his "trip," Ginsberg decides he is the Messiah, and starts trying to organize a "big cosmic electronic love talk" with a phone call to world leaders. "War is just a hang-up. We'll get the love-thing flowing on the electric Bell Telephone network." As the events of the last half-century have shown, this didn't work.

Drugs are completely illegal in China, and at least as far as I can tell, relatively rare. Burlington is considered somewhat of a "stoner" town (relatively speaking), so at home I was used to the idea that many of my students probably smoked pot. Almost all of them drank alcohol heavily, on a regular basis. The situation at GDUFS, however, was very different. The students I knew there didn't drink very often, and they certainly didn't take drugs. In fact, in Guangdong province I didn't see much public drinking at all.

In nice restaurants, you could hear men getting pretty drunk in private rooms, but out in the main dining area, Fred and I were almost always the only people in the restaurant ordering and drinking beer. This situation was even something of a joke among the foreign professors. We had many banquets organized on our behalf, and there were always lots of toasts, but the wine served was *only* for toasting. Waitresses would circle the table pouring about a quarter-inch of wine in each glass, and refilling it only after a formal toast had been made. One bottle of wine was usually enough to serve a table of eight for an entire meal. "Why can't they just once fill the glass?" an American colleague complained to me. When I traveled in Northern China, I saw people drink a lot more, but generally speaking people were extremely health-conscious and fit in Guangdong province.

The drug and alcohol use Leary described therefore was deeply unpopular with the students, and the acid rock I played in class, by the Beatles, Jimi Hendrix, Janis Joplin, etc., was greeted by wincing faces. For example, this student made it clear that she was not impressed by the story in the reading:

> Although drugs can take people into a "fancy" world, it seems to be a menace to me. From the descriptions of the experience of taking drugs we can see that the effects of drugs are very unpredictable. People may have illusions and even be insane. For example, after Allen took the drug, he considered himself as the Messiah, and attempted to call Kerouac in the name of God. He is obviously out of reason . . . So I think drugs is dangerous and should be regulated.

Students had other complaints as well; several thought that the anti-materialist claims of counter-culture adherents rang false:

> Born in an era of material affluence, some young rebels did question the value of rampant materialism. However, the way they voice their objection was also

hedonistic. If we took a closer look at the emblematic counterculture trinity (sex, drugs and rock and roll), it was obvious that all three offered a temporary ecstasy. It was doubtful that such ecstasy could guarantee spiritual fulfillment rather than emptiness afterwards. But the fact that drugs, especially the LSD, were used to construct a mental health by creating hallucinatory experience did indicate that their mental fulfillment, if there really was any, relied heavily on the materialistic condition. In this sense, young rebels themselves were more soaked in materialism instead of rebelling against it.

This was a fantastic Marxist critique of the "turn on" philosophy of baby boomers.

Voicing more traditional concerns, many students simply couldn't support how radically "counter" the counter-culture was:

Firstly . . . they failed to see the positive aspects of the society, such as the economic prosperity that offered many people comfortable life. Secondly, they were very radical, so much so that they abandoned all moral criteria to achieve what they want to get, which accounted for the fact that in later years many criminals and emotionally-disturbed young people were drawn to hippie communities. This is also one of the reasons that the counterculture movement gradually faded out of the history. Thirdly, the way they reacted against the mainstream society such as drug-taking and sexual promiscuousness brought about many social problems that American society was and is still trying to get rid of. Therefore, although the counterculture movement to a large extent liberated American society and contributed to its diversity and inclusivity, the negative impacts

resulted from it largely outweighed the positive
influences

After reading these negative reviews for Leary, et al., I was
interested to see if my students might instead be drawn to
those who vociferously railed against the excesses of the
counter-culture movement.

For our class the next week on the rise of the
Conservative movement, I asked Fred to join us for the day
and discuss what it was like growing up in a devoutly
Republican family in the 1960s. Fred had just arrived in
China for the first time, and had no idea how different my
classroom there was from the equivalent back home.
Consequently, he showed pictures of himself as a baby, being
strolled around Boston in a carriage covered with Barry
Goldwater stickers, and told my students about his family's
dinner-hour homilies on the evils of the Kennedys. Then he
asked them what were the political issues they discussed with
their own families at home? They seemed actually shocked
at the question.

"No, never politics!" a young woman shouted back,
and the students all agreed. "You didn't discuss any politics
with your family at dinner?" Fred asked my students, truly
surprised. The message about politics at home, they told him,
was "mind your own business and be quiet about that." This
message was not a surprise to me; my students' parents were
children of the 1960s, brought up in absolute fear of
government officials who might relocate your family to
brutal labor camps or back-breaking farms, torture you for
hanging the wrong picture on the wall or not hanging the
right one, and family, friends, and neighbors who might label
you a counter-revolutionary to resolve a grudge. What a
difference – their 1960s "cultural revolution" and ours.

At the end of the semester, I organized a karaoke
party for our class. I had wanted to put together a playlist of

1960s songs, but that proved to be too difficult. Instead, we had to rely on what was already available in the club's machines, which included some Frank Sinatra, Elvis, Beatles, and Simon and Garfunkel. The students were incredibly good at singing. They told me that they practiced the songs they would perform a lot before the party. I started trying to explain the karaoke scene in America in my limited experience, but stopped. I was about to belittle something they obviously took quite seriously. At one point, I was belting out a horrible rendition of some song I only half remembered the tune for, and one of my students picked up the other microphone and sang over me. He clearly wanted to help me save face. From my perspective, I was just performing karaoke like an American, for whom the purpose of the entertainment (it seems to me) is the bonding that comes from shared humiliation.

After an hour or so, everyone gave up on the English songs, and they used the rest of the party to sing their favorites – which were pretty much all romantic ballads in Mandarin and Cantonese. The running video loops featured young lovers, in tears, running through fields and often reconnecting on a bridge. One student got a bit weepy during a Cantonese love song. She told me that her mother had sang that to her as a little girl. "The mother tongue," she said, "you feel in your heart." I don't think she will be seeking out Jim Morrison tunes to add to her playlist any time soon.

The week following our karaoke party, I gave them their final exam. One of the questions they had to answer was:

One of the choices made by Americans in the 1960s era was whether to adopt counter-culture or conservative beliefs. Discuss the political and social attitudes and beliefs of these opposing groups, using specific examples. Which movement do you feel was

more correct, and why?
The final tally was 16 for counter-culture, and 8 for
conservative beliefs. That was not quite as liberal as my
Vermont students, but I thought it was still a pretty liberal
vote. On the pro-conservative side, students wrote chiefly in
opposition to drug use and a general loss of moral values:

- "The strategies and attitudes held by students of the
  counter-culture movement were radical and
  pessimistic . . . by degenerating themselves, they
  cannot reach the political goals so easily. In contrast,
  the conservative movement took steady and practical
  steps, with strong moral belief."
- 'Their ideas were too utopian, too idealistic, and some
  actions were too extreme such as drug abuse and
  promiscuous sex."
- "[Conservatives]" were not silent. They sticked
  strongly to the traditional values which they believed
  had led them to up and downs so many years. Their
  choice of traditional way of life had told everyone
  they were confident with themselves and with
  heritage from ancestors."
- "The conservative group's attitudes and beliefs were
  unfair to the Blacks and the unfortunate, but their
  actions were more beneficial to the social order and
  economic stability."

In contrast, the counter-culture camp found a variety of
positive reasons to support radical change:

- "Though I am agree with conservatives that personal
  struggle is important, I don't think any society,
  especially Capitalist ones could stay prosperous if a
  considerable proportion of people don't have the
  ability to consume. It is impossible to keep the
  production and consumption circle going in situations

like that."

- "The conservatives proposed a hierarchical society which lay so much stress on private property. It is in essence a retrogressive ideology."
- "The conservative and traditional way of life is believed to be lack of vitality."
- "I'm in favor of counter-culture beliefs for they espouse diversity, freedom, love, and peace. Significantly, these beliefs also impelled the government to think more than twice before making decisions."
- "Though such movements created tension in society, as Martin Luther King, Jr. said, the tension was "a necessary phase of transition." Unless those problems were solved, there could be no real stability." "

My students' answers on their final exam, of course, are not a reliable predictor of pretty much anything. But their answers do reveal a clash between traditional and ideological thinking about "social order" and proper behavior, and a passionate desire for liberty, respect for individuals, and social justice, which they associate with democratic (not socialist or Communist) principles.

Although many American baby boomers really did "tune out," many also became actively involved in politics, rising to dominate in the White House, governor's mansions, and state houses across the country. Many were mobilized to take over the halls of power. I was curious to know if some of my passionate students would have similar desire to become involved as "part of the solution" within the CPC. On many occasions, I heard diatribes about corruption, lack of input, deathly boring meetings, profiteering, and incompetent, lazy bureaucrats. Then, I would ask if the person was a party member, and the answer at least half the time was yes.

One of my brightest and most earnest students took the time to write me a lengthy e-mail about her experience as a party member:

> In my college classes, no one actually has real interest in becoming a party member, but every one knows that joining the party might be good for their career in China. However, the process to get in is somewhat complicated. I submitted my application in the last year of high school--actually I didn't want to, but my teacher urged me to apply, because he knew I had a good chance to get in. I took the test, which was about party knowledge, then I wrote tons of essays-- we call them "thought reports"--and I was interviewed by some senior party members, who asked me questions like "Why do you want to become a party member?" I forget what I said, but I remember I recited something from a textbook--actually just praising the party. As you can see, most aspects of the party are fake! . . . You must also have heard about boring party meetings. In fact, no one has real interest in attending the meeting, but if you skip one meeting, there will be records.

After reading this e-mail, I realized that no Chinese person had ever said anything nice to me about the Party – even and most especially all the members I knew. In fact, I only ever read nice things about the Party in sponsored propaganda or in articles in the Western press about the "amazing" growth in the economy.

When I suggested to a student I knew really well that there didn't seem to be much love for the Party, he said "Oh yes, but go out into the rural areas. There's lots of support there." But then, when I asked further: "Okay, but what about people your age in the rural areas?" Then, there was a hesitation. "Well, maybe not young people."

Those who were indoctrinated through terror to the point of espousing a cult-like adoration of Mao are old now. Today's rising students don't suffer from the collective Post Traumatic Stress Disorder their parents experienced as a result of China's Cultural Revolution – just as America's Baby Boomers hadn't lived through the Great Depression or World War II. One student I was talking to about the profound generation gaps in the country told me that the changing cultural situation made her mother in a rural area very upset. "She says that she can hardly know me."

Many American families in the 1960s felt this same disconnect. American counter-culture boomers weren't raised to become radical revolutionaries – instead, technology, affluence, new thinking, civil rights protests, and the idealism and camaraderie of youth all combined together to foment an explosive reaction. China's rising generation might not be willing to wear political tee-shirts just yet – but that doesn't mean it isn't going to happen.

If the CPC wants to raise the odds of its survival, at the very least, leaders should build a sense of inclusion among their own party members. If not public comment, then how about just party member comment? Why not let faculty members have some more control over the curriculum, to meet the changing needs and interests of the "vital blood" of the country? Whether they like it or not, China's leaders will be held to a very different standard in the coming years, in a climate in which many more ideas and aspirations are blowing in the wind.

Chapter Eight. Vietnam and the Powerful Example of American Democracy

One of the most surreal visions I experienced in China occurred during the first week of the fall term. Walking across campus in early September, I was stopped in my tracks by a platoon of students marching in front of me in formation, carrying rifles and dressed in army drab. After they passed by, I continued on towards my classroom, and discovered that across the campus, there were thousands of students marching in uniform, with sergeants alongside shouting orders. When I got to class, I asked my graduate students what was going on, and they smiled -- these were the incoming first-year students. For the first few weeks of college, almost every undergraduate in China's vast system of public universities endures military training.

Honestly, they looked like pathetic soldiers – skinny, bored, miserable. I would see them late in the afternoon, exhausted, sitting on benches and chatting, or lying flat out on the grass. They already knew how to march and perform basic drills before they got to college, since these are standard elements of physical exercise classes beginning in elementary school. Personally, I found it chilling to watch eight-year olds outside the school near our house, in formation, being chided for not standing at attention correctly. If this ever happened in our public schools in Burlington, Vermont, there would be hours of angry public comment at the school board -- it wouldn't happen twice.

This military orientation was especially surprising to

me because of its comparison to the "new student orientation" at Saint Michael's and other U.S. colleges like ours. When new students first arrive at Saint Michael's, staff and upper-class volunteers help families carry their belongings from SUVs and station wagons into the dorms, and sometimes reassure weepy parents and students suffering separation anxiety. In the evening, there is an inspiring program of lectures and music, at which the new students pledge academic honesty and other virtues. Upper-class students host games, parties, and outings designed to make sure that the new students feel welcome and happy, and make friends quickly. Throughout the first week, there are lots of whistles, horns, balloons, and magic marker "we love you" signs – but definitely no marching.

The difference between the college orientation weeks in China and the United States is suggestive of vast philosophical differences regarding adolescence, education, the relationship of the individual to the state, the role of the University, and of course, social privilege. Students in both countries need to situate themselves within new kinds of families when they go off to college or university, but in China the degree of disconnection from their past life is much more dramatic. I found it sad to learn that most of my Chinese students attend and graduate from university without ever enjoying a visit from their family members. Most parents and grandparents, I was told, can't take off from work, or don't have the money for a bus or train ticket, or simply are not used to leaving their home villages. In the recent past at GDUFS, there wasn't even much of a graduation ceremony – just the distribution of stamped certificates demonstrating completion of a degree.

Many of those past realities are changing. More families are buying cars, and the explosive growth of high-speed train lines in China is adding to the ease of moderately-priced travel. And at GDUFS, the new President told me that he was going to read the names of all 6,000 graduates that spring, and hand each one a diploma. Each of the Departments had its own ceremony as well, and distributed beautiful certificates worthy of framing. At graduation this year, the students I spoke to seemed both excited and grateful to have their names read out loud. Although most still did not have family members in attendance, they dressed up and took lots of photos with friends on the grounds of the campus – jumping, holding stuffed animals, and posing in campy hugs with the sculptures of Confucius, Shakespeare, and Beethoven in the GDUFS "Scholar's Garden." Beginnings and endings are more than symbolic; they shape our perceptions of experience, and assign value and meaning to our accomplishments. The President's personal touch has made him a huge celebrity among the students. This small but significant flourish is yet another sign that enthusiasm for Western humanism is escalating among China's rising generation – they want to be seen as individuals.

Nevertheless, there is nothing that can break down someone's sense of personal identity faster than military training, and this is where the future and the past collide (as so often happens in modern China). The fact that students still march and drill at GDUFS during their first month of college probably has something to do (at least remotely) with the country's long history of foreign invasions. Mongolians, Russians, Portuguese, British, Germans, and Japanese all invaded parts of what China believed to be its sovereign territory at different periods in its history. Those years of foreign invasion would appear to be over, but the CPC isn't taking any chances. The government is still engaged in a variety of disputes over land and sea rights with almost all of its eastern and southern neighbors, and it has clamped down hard on separatists in the West. As in Xinjiang province, the

Party message rings out from a huge number of proverbial signposts -- every Chinese person should be prepared to actively protect the homeland against foreign imperialists.

Although America has a much better historical track record in China than England or Japan, we are at the top of the list of Imperialists that Chinese children are often taught to fear. One graduate student took me aside after class and confided apologetically, "You know, we were told terrible things about America as children. But now I don't think they are true."

The historical relationship between our countries is indeed an intense and paradoxical mix. We were heroes and saviors for our anti-Japanese efforts in World War II, but also fierce adversaries in the Korean War. Currently both our countries use each other as foils in propaganda efforts. Although Chinese anti-American and anti-foreigner sentiment is written about a lot in the Western press, we mostly enjoyed huge smiles and gracious welcomes. In class, my students never expressed disgust for America, even when we talked about the atrocities of slavery, anti-Chinese legislation, civil rights era murders, etc. At the very least, even if they were disgusted, they were too polite to say so out loud.

In the less-public venue of their homework about U.S. topics however, the term "hypocritical" came up often. And one young man proudly presented statistics from the Chinese government's annual report on American human rights abuses in our 1960s class, including data on our income inequality, percentage of individuals lacking health insurance coverage, high incarceration and homicide rates, and education budget cuts (*touché*). These minor expressions of disapproval, however, were far from the norm.

In my classrooms, there was only one topic that really unnerved all of us, and released strong negative emotions about the United States -- the Vietnam War. Our unit on this topic led me to think in new ways both about the power of the example of American democracy, and the legacies of China's own difficult past.

The readings I assigned for this unit from *The Columbia Guide to the 1960s* included the following devastating facts:

- Tonnage of bombs dropped in Vietnam War: 7 million
- Tonnage of bombs dropped in World War II: 2 million
- Total defoliation of land in Vietnam, in acres, from 1962 to 1970: 5,182,307
- Gallons of herbicide used in Operation Ranch Hand in 1967: 4.8 million
- Gallons of Agent Orange used in Vietnam: 11,220,000
- Diseases that the Department of Defense originally recognized in 1992 as caused by dioxin, a chemical component of Agent Orange: Hodgkins' Disease, Non-Hodgkins lymphoma, soft tissue carcinoma, birth defects, chloracne."
- Total US deaths: 56,360
- Total Vietnamese deaths: 1.5 million

My lecture for the first class of the unit was a fairly straightforward year-by-year review of the war abroad and at home. I started with the end of French colonial rule in 1954, then covered the buildup of advisors and troops, the conflict's major military actions, the protests in the U.S., and then finished up with the story of the evacuation of the last American operatives when Saigon fell to Communist forces in April, 1975.

This is of course a complicated narrative; events both

far away and at home helped shaped the course of those chaotic years, as did the traumatic and dramatic histories of the four Presidents who led the country during that time (Eisenhower, Kennedy, Johnson, and Nixon). I showed iconic photographs, and tried to boil everything down as much as possible, to lay the foundation for the more intense readings of the next few weeks – including stories by Ron Kovic, Tim O'Brien, and David Lance Goines. This foundation also was critically important for understanding the counter-culture movement, and the rise of conservatism.

The students were dutifully quiet during my slide show. They didn't seem to know too much about the Vietnam War. For fifty years, China has denied any involvement in aiding its Communist neighbors during the war (the relationship between China and Vietnam is even more complicated than between our countries), so it isn't presented as their battle against us.

The week before, we had a series of fun team presentations on subjects like mini-skirts, Bob Dylan, and Betty Friedan, and I hadn't given a formal lecture in a while. The students now were used to more interactive pedagogy. It was a relief for them, then, when I finished my PowerPoint presentation and introduced my parents who were sitting in the back of the classroom. They were touring China and Southeast Asia for a month, and stayed in Guangzhou with us for two weeks. Neither had any teaching experience, but they agreed that it would be fun to talk about their own experiences as Americans living through the 1960s.

Married in 1960, Glenda and Harvey Werbel "spent most of the decade changing diapers," as my mother likes to point out. My father was a young lawyer in Brooklyn at the time, and my mother worked part time as a speech pathologist. They didn't listen to the Beatles' White album, or take psychedelic drugs. In fact, they didn't have much in common with any of the activists and leaders we were reading about at the time, and therefore were a good example of the complexities of American opinion during the decade. Like many Americans, they spent the 1960s absorbed in their own lives, filtering events through the lens of personal involvement, and somewhat detached from the commotion. I put a picture on the screen of my parents in the mid-1960s – my father with thick black plastic glasses and his hair slicked back, and my mother in a miniskirt with her hair piled on top of her head in a huge chignon. I invited them to come up to the front of the room, and the students all applauded, and seemed genuinely happy to meet my family.

Initially, the questions were fairly straightforward: "Did you think that wearing a miniskirt was a feminist statement?" My mother's answer was that she hadn't really thought about it like that, but her decision to go to graduate school and pursue a profession definitely felt like a rebuttal to her father's vision that she would become strictly a housewife. "What did you think of the presidential candidates?" They said that they had a lot of respect for Johnson, thought Barry Goldwater was a terrible Presidential candidate, and never trusted Nixon. But mostly they didn't get too involved in politics, and they thought the protests were upsetting and dangerous. "What did you think about the war?" My parents replied that they did not support the war, and didn't really know too many people who did. The mostly young middle-class people they knew did a variety of things to avoid the draft. My father was fortunate to have completed his military service between the Korean and Vietnam Wars, on an army base in New Jersey. They didn't know any of the combat troops in Vietnam. But they also had to admit that they didn't do much to assert their anti-war point-of-view. They were at home, "changing diapers."

Towards the end of class, a young woman in the

middle of the room stood, her voice shaking with emotion, and asked them: "How can you call yourselves a representative democracy? You say that people didn't like the war, but then the government went ahead anyway!" Her assertion was technically wrong, because the reading had done a pretty good job of demonstrating that polls indicated that the public did favor the war (by a small margin) throughout most of the 1960s. Despite the mistake though, it was still an interesting question, both because of her unusual public display of emotion, and her demand to know how the Vietnam War squared with my parents' understanding of what living in a democracy meant.

My upset student was not alone in her feelings. Over the course of the next few weeks, many students demonstrated confusion about the function and procedures of democracy as they tried to make sense of the Vietnam War. This was especially true as we listened to protest songs, saw video clips of demonstrations in which students were beaten, bloodied, and even shot, and read first-hand accounts by veterans and activists. In their homework assignments, the students typically tried to see all this through a positive lens, despite the flood of so many grim statistics:

> With their basic rights to vote, to speak, and to assembly, people, from all walks of life, are much concerned with politics. They have a sense of social responsibility. When the Vietnam War triggered opposition at home, Colleges students conducted sit-ins to express their concern. Even the pop songs in the Sixties conveyed antiwar messages. By participating in national affairs, American people become the masters of their country. I believe a pursuit for freedom and equality, and a high rate of public participation in national affairs are what make America a democratic country.

Another student similarly waxed poetic about our idealistic form of government:

> As stated in the <u>Declaration of Independence</u>, "all men are created equal," and "governments are instituted among men" to guarantee human rights. Individualism is an American tradition that always takes rights of individual as priority. For instance, although the government justified the Vietnam War as necessary for the security of the nation, American people launched Anti-Vietnam War Movement in spite of being criticized as unpatriotic. Actually, all movements in 1960s demonstrate American's belief that rights if individual comes before government.

Another student even bothered to get out her dictionary:

> . . . According to Merriam-Webster dictionary, "democracy" means government by the people of rule of majority. During the short history of the America in the 1960s, there were several examples to show how the supreme power was vested in the people, and how it had been exercised directly or indirectly through a system of representation usually including periodically held free election. During this period, a lot of movements took place to change the society and make progress, such as Civil Rights movement, anti-war movement, Free Speech movement, and Women's movement, etc. . . . The movements were all started by common people, and through non-violent means. They achieved what they demanded through the changing of legislation and government policy . . . In a word, Americans don't like to be limited, and they will fight for freedom all the time . . . The reason why so many people at home went against the Vietnam War must have some relation with their independence complex. American people

today are also famous for their independent virtue. These effusive summations of our "freedom," "equality," and "independent virtue," were not in any way nuanced, but they were consistent. The Mandarin word for America -- *Meiguo* -- literally means "beautiful country," and in keeping with the appellation, my Chinese students tended to see us, and especially our democratic form of government, through *Meiguo*-colored glasses.

By contrast, my lectures, with their pictures of Phan Thi Kim Phuc (the naked girl suffering napalm burns in a famous photo), the My Lai massacre, wounded American soldiers, and defeated political operatives clinging to a rising helicopter, allowed little room for window-dressing. Our class discussions, therefore, were much more fraught. This wasn't history – even American history -- as they were used to studying it. As my dictionary-quoting student wrote, the American story is supposed to be about the triumph of democratic values over evil. She was not alone in her view. Another student wrote:

> In retrospect, all the movements or counter-culture forces were persuing the same goal [of freedom and equality] by and large. For example, the anti-war movement started mainly from campus, the young people just found that the Vietnam War was just against the fundamental doctrine and creed of this country. They found that the war was a mistake and the government just drove against the will of the world for peace and freedom.

What my students couldn't quite grapple with was that most Americans actually voted for those who continued our involvement in Vietnam, and many in fact believed that fighting godless Communists was at the heart of the nation's "creed."

The protest movement was powerful, to be sure, but it

wasn't effective enough to save the tens of thousands of
Americans, or millions of Vietnamese who were killed or
wounded (not to mention the long-term effects of defoliating
much of a nation with agricultural poisons). But these
statistics didn't make it into the students' assessments of
America in the 1960s. In fact, only one student really went
beyond a jazzed-up, happy narrative, and explained the
situation with insightfulness and clarity in his homework.

> The majority of American people considered antiwar
> protestors as unpatriotic or even traitorous because
> for them it seemed that if you loved your country
> enough you should have faith in your mother country
> and in what it was doing. Actually, before the
> Vietnam War, America had always performance as an
> embodiment of justice, from the American War for
> Independence to the Second World War. And
> America had always won, which was also in accord
> with people's belief in the triumph of Good over Evil.
> Thus most American people were still waiting for the
> victory in this war to strengthen their confidence in
> their country. But to those antiwar protestors, whose
> number increased as the war proceeded, patriotism
> meant fighting for the good of the country and
> stretching out for justice. They saw their loss in the
> Vietnam War and wanted to put an end to it, which,
> to my understanding, is a more rational kind of
> patriotism.

In this student's summation, the country was split between
those waiting for the mythic narrative of a perfect America to
repeat itself, and those who were willing to see "the loss . . .
and put an end to it." Admitting "the loss" was indeed more
rational, as the Pentagon Papers later demonstrated, but
painfully inconsistent with our nation's usual self-
aggrandizement.

In retrospect, I think what some of my students found upsetting and / or simply hard to integrate in this unit was that they expected us to be better than we were. In their eyes, democracy--with its open participation, free speech guarantees, and majority rule--sounds so good that of course it should produce "virtuous" government. Our political *rhetoric* is truly worthy of the designation *Meiguo*. My students' didn't expect China to be like America, but they expected America to be like their vision of America. When government "by the people" produced bad, irrational decisions, it ran against their expectations, and frankly, was a big disappointment.

Throughout the class, my students credited democracy for the gains of the Civil Rights movement, the improved legal and social status of women and Native Americans, etc., They saw those developments as great examples of instances when free people stood up and said what they believed, and ameliorated injustice. In their idealistic view, all of our scourges could be solved with more democracy. But of course, representative democracy can produce epic failures (like the Vietnam War) as well as epic victories (like the Civil Rights Act). The difference involves not only rational thinking, but also a willingness to critically examine and reject the ideological and nationalistic presentations of history that so often blind policy makers.

Coming to terms with epic national failures in the historical past requires concerted effort by participants, scholars, artists, and citizens. My students had the opportunity to read some of that painful work written by soldiers and activists in the decade following the war. The grim task of processing historical tragedy of course has been taken up by generations of brilliant humanists, who have attempted to explain, or at least derive meaning from evils committed in countries including Germany, Japan,

Cambodia, South Africa, and Rwanda. In America, some of our greatest works of fiction, art, and film have helped the nation process our tragic involvement in the conflicts in Southeast Asia.

In China, writers, filmmakers, and artists also have grappled with the atrocities of the Communist regime, most notably the Great Leap Forward and the Cultural Revolution. But the CPC's answer to the question of what to do with this history has been an appalling combination of propagandistic lies and silencing of the truth. Some of those brave enough to try and make sense of these past horrors have been censored, forced into exile, jailed, or worse. Chinese people are not supposed to "see the loss," but are required to keep returning to the memorized sayings of Mao and Deng Xiaoping, and to "history" books sanitized by committees willing to publish only the most celebratory accomplishments of the Party. The government's willingness to describe Mao as "two-thirds right and one- third wrong" isn't going lead to the same reconciliation as if they let people publicly discuss their own stories – especially since these stories are ubiquitous -- seared indelibly across the landscape of the country.

For my very first lecture trip, I traveled to Shantou, on the southeastern coast of China, about 270 miles from Guangzhou. It was October, and still fairly warm. Shantou University is more Westernized than others that I visited. The professors are mostly expats, and the facilities have been funded by more than 700 million US dollars in donations from a wealthy Hong Kong businessman named Li Ka-shing. The University is something of an experimental partnership between the Chinese government and its (somewhat) foreign partner.

My lectures for Law and Journalism students went extremely well; the rooms were packed, and the questions were interesting. The tour of the city and surrounding areas was less thrilling. I thoroughly enjoyed my companions, a boisterous and friendly group, but the city itself was something of a dud. The sky and buildings were mostly gray, and older sites largely had been destroyed, making way for a sea of concrete slab buildings. One of the professors confided to me that Shantou's claim to fame (or lack thereof) is that it is the Special Economic Zone that never gained the wealth of Shenzhen, Xiamen, or any of the other cities specifically retooled to attract foreign investment.

The most interesting place I saw on the tour was the massive residence of a business tycoon named Chen Ci Hong, who made a fortune in Thailand in the early 20th century, and built a 500-room mansion filled with architectural details reflecting his worldly travels. European tiles, Chinese roofs and courtyards, and Southeast Asian woodcarvings all harmoniously were incorporated into the sprawling design.

Although the architectural details were interesting, and the extraordinary wealth of the family was amply demonstrated in the text of the wall panels, the house conveyed mostly an ominous, dark aura. The furniture was gone, and the dusty, dry land surrounding the house seemed barren. Over all the doors and windows in the interior of the house, someone had stenciled the iconic, smiling face of Mao, wearing his trademark military cap, and cheerfully looking up and to the side. Enormous wooden gates barred the doorways that previously had led to the bedrooms of wives, concubines, and children. Chen and his family had wisely fled from China in the 1940s rather than live under Communist rule.

In their absence, the mansion had been confiscated and used as a prison for "counter-revolutionaries." The Mao paintings were part of the indoctrination program, stenciled above all the windows and doors where prisoners (people like professors, doctors, landowners, etc.) were held. I tried to imagine how they might have felt about that face, beaming from above every potential exit out of hell. The text panels referred only to the years the house was a prison – there was no discussion of how many inmates had been held there, or any of the names of the prisoners. The history lesson simply stopped when Chen fled. The CPC may want to erase the past, but as in Shantou the scars of that awful period are ubiquitous. Traveling around the country today, one sees the damage everywhere – from painted Maos, to purposefully damaged ancient paintings and sculpture in temples, to tourist attractions that have been "restored" from the ground up because they were demolished.

Chinese people live in this landscape, in the shadow of this era, and with its stories and memories never far from the surface. The effort to suppress all of that for the sake of national face is enormous, and of course the task is hopeless in light of all the obvious evidence. The contrast with how Americans grapple with history is stark.

When I presented the grim facts of the Vietnam War, I think it really upset some of the students because I gave my own country bad face. I taught the ugly history of my own government, and gave them proof in a variety of media that large numbers of Americans publicly and passionately supported inhumane actions. Although I panicked when some of my students turned hostile on my unwitting parents, in retrospect, I didn't need to be worried. My father was unfazed.

When the young woman angrily demanded that my parents explain how Americans can call their nation a democracy, he shrugged his shoulders, put his hands on his hips, and responded, "So, we made a mistake. It happened, and it was a tragedy. We were wrong. But doesn't every country make mistakes? Is your government so perfect?"

The class responded with a hushed tone. She stammered, "no, I guess, of course not." "Is any government perfect?" he continued. It was a simple question, but in China, the answer is complicated.

Without belaboring the point, and with great and succinct clarity, what my father was implicitly arguing was a kind of reconciliation with your country's past. Being *Meiguo* doesn't mean that we always act like M*eiguo*. By turning my student's question back to her, he challenged the whole class to consider "well, what if your history isn't so great either? What are you going to do with that?" This wasn't the kind of conversation my students were used to having in history class.

In America, we enjoy an incredible freedom to investigate, analyze, and express our ideas about the past. Debates over our country's history and its future can be heard in every corner of the nation, from kitchen tables and downtown diners to the halls of Congress. Thanks to institutions like the Library of Congress and the National Archives, and to laws like the Freedom of Information Act, we have access to remarkable amounts of source material to fuel the endless dialogue that takes place in our Universities as well as the offices of policy makers. Without allowing that kind of cathartic public conversation, it's hard to imagine how any government can win the trust of its people, or how any people can dream of living up to their most idealistic historical narratives. Informed dialogue is the only shot we have at making government "by the people" "virtuous." And hopefully, some of my students will take away from this unit that our public debate is a vital part of what makes us *Meiguo*, even if it is often very ugly and frequently frustrating.

Chapter Nine. Teaching and Practicing Sisterhood: The Women's Rights Movement

In January, when my delightful visit to Chen village in Foshan was concluding, Mary and her mom accompanied me part of the way back to Guangzhou on the train. As we stood on the crowded metro, holding on to the poles for balance, Mary translated a question her mother wanted to ask: "Was it true that I had children, in addition to being a professor?" Of course, I was more than happy to pull out my collection of wallet photographs of Graham and Emmett, from adorable chubby babies with blond curls and big blue eyes, to full-grown men. Mrs. Chen beamed back at me, and then at Mary. Mary later told me that her mother was extremely skeptical about the possibility that her daughter could get married and have a child, given her plans for graduate school and a career. She was already twenty-four, and so the pressure was on not to become what is known as a "leftover" (unmarried) woman. Mary was glad I could reassure her. Not only was I able to become a professor, but also to have the good fortune of two sons.

Despite the language barrier, this was a moment of bonding between Mrs. Chen and myself as mothers, one that had the added benefit of helping out a young woman with her family's anxieties. Mrs. Chen smiled broadly at my baby pictures, and nodded her head. As mothers, our pride and worry connected us instantaneously despite the huge gulf that divided us in terms of language, culture, and life experiences. One of my greatest realizations of the year was that this brand of soft power – connecting with other women and other mothers -- was the most trenchant, and poignant, in my diplomatic arsenal. In that regard, one of my initial losses turned out to be a great win.

My Dean at GDUFS was a lovely man in his early forties, who exuded bright charm from his short, slim frame. Our initial contact via e-mail while I was still in America was somewhat tense. One of the most difficult aspects of being a Fulbright scholar, particularly in China, is finding out quite late what you will teach. I didn't get any information about my department until early July, and then the Dean didn't end up finalizing my teaching roster until August, at which point we were moving – which gave me little time for advance preparation.

The process of getting my course roster was a great example of how most things happened in China. I wrote to the Dean via e-mail that I would like to teach the courses proposed in my Fulbright application – a graduate seminar on American Culture from the Civil War to World War I, and another on America in the 1960s. He responded that would be fine, and then a week later asked if I could also give a few lectures for undergraduates on American art which would "broaden their horizons."

I agreed to that readily, thinking this would not be too much work since I wouldn't have to grade papers or exams. A few days later, though, he wrote back again to say that the Vice Dean thought that attendance would be better for the undergraduate course if they could take it for credit. I realized then that he was negotiating for a better deal. I thought about this one quite a bit, and decided to negotiate back. I agreed to the third course (even though Fulbrighters are only supposed to teach two per semester) as long as I could have teaching assistants assigned to help me. That was no problem. But the "negotiations" weren't over. By the time we were done, I had been assigned to teach two graduate seminars and not one but two sections of the undergraduate course. I had been out-bargained, and it would not be the last time by a long shot.

A week before school began, I received the contact information for my teaching assistants – two Master's students, Charlotte and Ellen – who would help with my undergraduate lecture course sections (each of which had about thirty students). I wrote to them immediately, and invited them to join me for lunch the week before class began.

My lunch with Charlotte and Ellen was pleasant, although a bit embarrassing for me since I wasn't yet used to the veneration professors in China receive from students. They both were effusively grateful for the "honor" of this (unpaid) assignment, but had no idea what it meant to be a teaching assistant. I explained the American system – in exchange for my mentoring them as young academics and taking them out to lunch often, they would grade the quizzes and serve as interpreters for students confused by my English language lectures. I had to firmly put an end to their demands that I allow them to pay the tab for lunch, as a sign of their respect. My trump card always was "this is the way we do things in America."

My relationship with Charlotte and Ellen proved to be extremely beneficial on all sides through the course of the year. We had lunch together every two weeks and discussed everything from teaching methodologies and grading standards to how to dress to gain the respect of students as an authoritative figure in the classroom. They, in turn, gave me enormous help in changing my lecture style to suit the young sophomores and juniors who were struggling to understand the class.

Following their advice, I added word definitions to each lecture, and many more slides of text. I also stopped lecturing every ten minutes or so, put a picture and question up on the power point slide, and gave the students a chance to discuss and practice an answer in Chinese with their neighbors before calling on them to respond in English. That small change eased their anxiety about speaking publicly in class, and made a big difference in student comprehension, although I can't say I was all too sure about that in the end. On their final exams for the semester, many students simply regurgitated chunks of the textbook from memory. It wasn't plagiarizing, exactly, but it also didn't inspire confidence that they had any idea what they were writing about. I couldn't blame them. Studying an entirely new discipline (art history) from a foreign culture and in a foreign language was certainly a tough triple whammy for nineteen- and twenty-year old students.

In addition to serving a somewhat official role as mentor to Charlotte and Ellen, I also developed close relationships with two female PhD candidates I met at the beginning of the year, which were much more interesting and intense. The two had tremendously different personalities. Cheryl was a bubbly, effusive woman in her early thirties. She had a broad face, arching eyebrows, a slender waist, long legs, and was taller than most Chinese women. Frilly and glittery outfits, and fashionable shoes complemented her natural beauty. Cheryl smiled more easily and frequently than anyone I have ever met, and laughed effusively at the slightest provocation. In short, she was a joy to be around.

Alice, in contrast, was an odd mix of bristling energy and earnest warmth, sometimes punctuated by moments of seeming incomprehension. I wasn't always sure that she knew what I was saying, and she definitely didn't find the humor in my jokes as easily as Cheryl. Some of the disconnect probably can be attributed to how busy and distracted she was. In addition to working on her PhD thesis,

Alice was teaching at two different universities, leading Communist Party activities for students, and she had long commutes between her home, work, and school. Alice was from a Northern province, and married to an executive with a large state-owned company. The couple clearly had great prospects, due to strong Party connections, and hard work.

After several conversations about shared interests, we developed a regular plan of lunches outside the gates of the University, typically at one of the Hunan restaurants that offered spicier food. When the three of us would go out to lunch, we always required that Alice choose the menu. As someone who had been party (literally) to great banquets and the dining habits of the informed and wealthy, Alice had eaten the best food in China. Under her supervision, the waiters delivered whole steamed fish topped with fresh chilis, garlic, soy, and cilantro. Lotus root arrived -- sliced, stuffed, and then braised in a rich bean-infused broth. We ate seared greens with fresh ginger, and delicate fried pumpkin cakes.

Eating brightened up every aspect of our lunches, and as the weeks passed and the beautiful courses arrived, we began to talk more about our personal lives. Cheryl and Alice both had two-year old boys. I showed my pictures of Graham and Emmett, and talked about how happy they were to be in China for the year. I also confessed my exhaustion at trying to stop the boys from fighting, and trying to discipline Emmett as an excessively cheeky adolescent. With Fred in the U.S. for the first few months, I didn't have any backup, and parenting them on my own was very stressful.

Cheryl talked about her situation at home with just one rambunctious boy, and plenty of help. She was married to a handsome young English professor from the North of China. Her marriage had caused some problems because her mother didn't approve of Cheryl marrying a boy from the "uncultivated" rural North. Nevertheless, Cheryl was in love, and she and her husband lived in an apartment downtown with his mother, who took care of their adorable son "Max" during the day, and did all the shopping, cooking, and laundry. There were some issues and complaints at home regarding standards of cleaning and food, but overall the arrangement was mutually beneficial, and followed everyone's expectations. The mother-in-law was looking forward to going back to her home village when Max went to school (and so was Cheryl).

At the end of Cheryl's story, and the passing of her photos, I asked about Alice's son, at which point she burst into tears. Cheryl put her arm around her friend, and spoke softly to her in Chinese. Then, Alice poured her heart out. Her son was basically being held captive by her parents in a Northeastern province. Her father was a powerful and rich local official, and her mother emphatically insisted that Alice couldn't raise a son properly if she was working, so the young boy had to stay with them. So, they had the boy far away, and Alice didn't get to see him very often. He was even learning to speak a different dialect from his father, who had been raised in the South.

The story may sound ridiculous to Americans – how could her parents essentially hold their grandchild hostage? But the women I met in China were far more weighted down by family expectations than my own students – especially by the tradition of *xiao dao,* respecting and caring for parents, which has been a core pillar of Confucianism and Chinese society for more than two thousand years. Alice simply couldn't face up to refusing her parents' demand.

Cheryl and I promptly comforted and commiserated with Alice (your parents are so wrong!), and bolstered her confidence that she could in fact work and take care of her son. By that point in our relationship, the three of us were girlfriends, not professional acquaintances. Our bonds as women and mothers were powerful.

In addition to the privilege of getting to know my wonderful teaching assistants well, and serving as a friend and academic mentor to Cheryl and Alice during the course of the year in various ways, I also had the joy of teaching a large number of young Chinese women, both undergraduates and Master's candidates in English. Many of these young women were outspoken when we discussed gender issues in class units, and many of them also sought me out during office hours to talk further about their relationships with parents, girlfriends, and men, as well as the expectations they held for their lives ahead as workers, wives, and mothers. These were the most interesting and surprising conversations of my year, because they often made me feel as though I were in some kind of time warp. On many occasions, I felt as though I was reliving a scene from Betty Friedan's *Feminine Mystique* -- the text students read for our coverage of the American Women's Liberation movement.

First published in 1963, Friedan's *Feminine Mystique* is widely credited for launching second-wave feminism in the United States, which focused on consciousness-raising about sexism in public and private spheres, as a first step towards legal and policy changes. The "first wave" of American feminism was led by Elizabeth Cady Stanton and Susan B. Anthony, who campaigned for suffrage and other basic legal rights; today's "third wave" feminists critique media stereotypes, and work pragmatically on problems that prevent women from enjoying the same opportunities and successes as men, such as inadequate and expensive day care options, and unequal expectations, treatment, and pay.

As many critics have noted, Friedan's timing was great. Simone de Beauvoir already had laid the intellectual foundations for the second wave with her book *The Second*

Sex, which demonstrated that gender was socially constructed and so could be reconstructed on a more even plane. Then, in 1960, the FDA approved birth control pills, and many women began to think about sex as decoupled from the burdens of childbearing. The pill made the sexual revolution possible. Friedan was a housewife in suburban New York City when she read de Beauvoir's text. She had graduated from Smith College, become involved in a variety of liberal political causes, and then married and bore primary responsibility for raising three children while her husband, an advertising executive, went off to work each day.

As a research project for a potential freelance writing piece, Friedan interviewed her Smith classmates around the time of their 15th College reunion, and found that, despite their conventional success as affluent housewives, her cohort suffered from a "problem that had no name" -- a "strange stirring, a sense of dissatisfaction, a yearning." Baking the perfect bread and keeping a tidy house was not making motivated and intelligent women happy. Instead, many felt depressed and isolated. Friedan realized that she and many of her classmates wanted to be the ones who left the house in the morning for a career in the city.

Response to Friedan's text was explosive, and women from all walks of life joined together to insist on change. They didn't get everything they wanted by a long shot, but American women did benefit enormously. In the years following *The Feminine Mystique*, Congress passed Title VII of the Civil Rights Act of 1964, which prohibits employment discrimination based on race, color, religion, sex, or national origin; and created the Equal Employment Opportunity Commission in 1965, as an enforcement mechanism for claims on the basis of Title VII. In 1972, the legislature additionally passed Title IX of the Education Amendments of 1972, which protects people from discrimination based on sex in education programs and activities that receive federal financial assistance.

When I teach *The Feminine Mystique* in Vermont, Friedan's description of American womanhood reads like an historical relic. In class discussions, my female students often pronounce that they will choose to stay home with their own children (like their mothers, or more commonly and pointedly *unlike* their mothers), but they never question whether they have a choice. I like to point out to my students that economic realities have more control over these possibilities than "choice," per se, but nonetheless the idea that America's female college students can succeed at whatever they decide to do is powerful, and an enormous change from the scene pre-1963.

My female Chinese college students also felt that they could make some choices, but those seemed often to be much harder and more complicated. Many women I met in China complained to me about forms of discrimination that are unimaginable in the United States. On employment applications, men and women are required to provide information on their marital status, weight, and height. Bosses can end an interview abruptly if they feel a young woman is not attractive enough, and many companies are not interested in hiring female office personnel who are married (and therefore might require some time off to give birth).

Mostly, women told me that they loved their bosses and colleagues and felt no discrimination, so I don't want to overstate the problem as I heard it. However, it still is true that in China, there is no EEOC to appeal to. Harassed women can choose to either play by unfair rules, or quit. A beautiful colleague in the Business department at GDUFS complained to me bitterly about leaving her high-paying post at a Chinese business firm because of the expectation that she would drink excessively with clients at banquets and make sure they were "happy."

The discrimination women face in American workplaces may be similar in some respects, but more egregious behaviors like these at least create liability for companies, thanks in large part to the legislative and policy changes demanded by women of Freidan's generation. Most of my American women students tell me that they definitely are not feminists, but when we study this history, and review the policies second wave feminists advocated for, they always agree that of course those were necessary and fair changes. American women now utterly take for granted the protections Chinese women still are years away from gaining.

Although discrimination undoubtedly is an egregious problem in China, it was relatively rare that women expressed this as a concern when discussing their future careers. Instead, the most pressing problems they discussed with me were family relationships and obligations. Parents wanted and expected their children to marry soon after graduating, and often put a lot of pressure on their daughters to move back to home provinces. Most of my students were only children, and so were facing the very real prospect that to carry forward the tradition of *xiao dao*, they would have to care for their own parents, as well as their husband's. Nothing has wreaked havoc with Chinese family structure more than the one-child policy, and there is a great deal of worry in China now about the coming crisis of care for a large population of sixty-somethings, with few children to share the burden of caring for them.

In class, when I discussed American controversies over the legality and funding for birth control and abortions, students seemed utterly flabbergasted. In China, birth control is pretty much required for sexually active women since it is illegal to have more than one child, and abortions are extremely common. There are some exceptions to this rule -- ethnic minorities, for example, can have two children -- but in general, if a family can't afford the $40,000 fine for having a second child (more or less depending on the province), they have few options, and none of them are good.

Outside of class, women spoke to me with enormous sadness about their desire for a second child, and some that I knew were actively trying to save up the money to pay the fine. This situation regarding family "planning" choices was unimaginable in the United States in the era of Friedan, as it is today. No "liberty" hits home for women more deeply than the choice to become a mother (or not). And our own utterly different, religion-fueled conversation about these issues is almost impossible to explain in China. I found that particular cultural translation to be a complete failure.

My American students also take for granted the helpful, frank discussions about sexuality, sexually-transmitted diseases, and birth control that are ubiquitous in America, whether in liberal middle- and high-school programs, or on the Internet. Chinese colleagues and students complained to me bitterly in private that young people were uninformed about these issues, largely due to censorship. One female undergraduate student came to my office on several occasions to ask frank questions about various forms of birth control. She also wanted to know how to enjoy sex, which she wanted to experience as soon as possible following graduation, when she planned to leave China for a study abroad opportunity.

I showed her the webpages on birth control and sexually transmitted diseases at www.mayoclinic.com, and gave her the same advice I give to students at home – be safe and have fun, and if you are in a relationship that takes you out of your comfort zone, or makes you feel disempowered or threatened in any way, get out of it. Ultimately, feeling somewhat embarrassed about the sex talk, I directed her to the website of *Cosmopolitan Magazine*. Helen Gurley Brown, who edited the magazine from 1965 until 1997, was the first woman in America to popularize frank sex talk that emphasized women's fun and satisfaction as well as men's. Her book, *Sex and the Single Girl*, published in 1962, changed the American dialogue about sex forever.

When I opened my browser to the homepage for *Cosmopolitan* in May to show my student the link, it featured articles including "99 Sex Questions: We answer the naughtiest things on your mind," and "How to crank up your sexual energy." Even if I could read Mandarin, I'm pretty sure these are not headlines I'd see on the cover of Chinese magazines. The fact is, in China, there hasn't been and still isn't anyone like Helen Gurley Brown. One student referenced the lack of radical voices on these issues in her homework assignment on *The Feminine Mystique*:

> As a matter of fact, there is no "radical women" in China mainland. And it is hard for me to find any evidence or information on Internet because feminists in China do not advocate "freedom of love," "freedom of marriage," or "freedom of government." They are limited in literature or philosophy as one "feminist" I found out in Internet said in 1992 when the Fourth World Woman Conference was held in Beijing, "I do not favor the earlier feminist project in the West. I want to establish a society in China men and women are equal and in harmony." I think it is very interesting to find out there is no "radical woman" in China.

Despite all the advantages women enjoy in America because of the Women's Liberation Movement of the 1960s

and 1970s, nevertheless, when we analyze the present
situation in class, it also is clear that second-wave feminism
was definitely not completely successful. For the second
class of this unit, we reviewed statistics on gender
differentials in America for the year 2011:

- Women held 17% of seats in the U.S. House and
  Senate, 22% of statewide elected offices, and 23% of
  seats in State legislatures.
- There were 6 women Governors.
- Of the largest 100 cities in America, 7 had women
  mayors.
- The United States ranked 72nd in the world in
  women's political representation.
- Around the world, women accounted for 19% of
  elected officials.
- Of the "Fortune 500" companies, 12 were run by
  women CEOs. (The highest-ranking of these
  companies run by a woman was 39th.)
- In 2010, women were 48% of graduates from medical
  school, 47% of law students, and roughly 30% of
  MBA students.

After I displayed each bullet-point statistic, I asked if this
seemed like "enough equality"? Only two boys sitting off on
their own said they were all fine (in a jocular burst of
humor). The women resolutely disagreed – these numbers all
seemed unfairly skewed, with the exception of recent
graduation rates.

 I then placed the students into groups and asked them
to choose the single most important statistic to focus on
balancing in order to create an equitable society: elected
officials, wages earned, CEOs of major companies,
professional school graduates, or caregivers for elderly,
children, and domestic chores. The students overwhelmingly
picked elected officials (I lean more towards caregiving and

domestic chore balance myself). Regardless of the rank order of the statistics, the demonstration was just as effective in China as it is in the United States. If you define "feminist" as someone who thinks that numbers like these aren't good enough, then everyone in the room usually leaves at least willing to rethink their membership in the feminist club.

At the end of class in China, I asked my students if they thought the statistics regarding gender and pay, politics, and workplaces were similar in both our countries, and my students had to think for a while. They thought things in China were definitely better for women than in other countries in Asia, because there aren't operative religious ideologies that are oppressive to women as there are in many other places. Also, the Communist party emphasizes equality between the sexes in much of its platform and policies. But, in reality, the students had to admit, there aren't many women in the highest ranks of the central government. Similarly, women run few businesses, although there now are a few famous female billionaires in China, including media mogul Yang Lan (sometimes referred to as "China's Oprah"). My students generally thought that China still seemed very much like a man's world. Their homework on Friedan reflected that, and many voiced concerns remarkably similar to those of my young women students in America.

One student asked whether Friedan was fair to place all her emphasis on women's need to evolve:

> Both man and woman should be responsible for the secondary role women played in the society. Firstly, women were misled by the conception that man and woman are simply different and they should conform to the traditional role that they should be a feminine being. Even if they realize the idea of "education", "independence" and "equality with man", they would be afraid to be labeled "unfeminine". Also they would

try to deny the dissatisfied voice within themselves in pursuit of femininity. That's why "the chains that bind her in her trap are chains in her own mind and spirit." But To a large extent, man should shoulder more responsibility for the circumstance. Because it is they who set the stereotype for woman. Women were taught by thousands of experts to be feminine and undesirous of careers, higher education, political rights. Most of the experts are men and the aim is to satisfy men's expectation and desire. Men monopolize most of the social resources. Therefore, they take control of almost every field and women's brains remain the most valuable but unexplored treasure in the world. So men overweigh women and rule them, even in a very subtle way. In this sense, both sexes, especially man should be responsible for woman's secondary role to man's.

In essence, this young woman was stating her position squarely in the camp of third-wave feminists.

Gender is a social construction, and that is equally true for women and for men. So, why shouldn't men be the ones to re-define themselves in a way to let women empower and define themselves? A young man in the class wrote from the same more 21st century perspective:

All the conceptions instilled into women were nothing but that they should care no other things but their family, relatives and all the domestic affairs. What if men are taught to devote their lives totally to careers and leave others things such as their families alone? I think the result may be the same as the problem of the women then, which means that also more and more men are going to see the doctors and want more than careers. What is subtle is that the requests of man not only involve a successful career, but also a happy family and some romantic moods; however on the contrary women then were constrained merely to the family. In a patriarchal society, that is not weird I think. Just as Simone De Beauvoir had written in *The Second Sex* that "One is not born, but rather becomes a woman", the whole society had successfully put the false conceptions into women's mind so that even women themselves had not realized the wrong conceptions but accepted them.

My male student here was willing to admit that "patriarchal" society, if genders were reversed, would be equally unfair to men -- which is essential to the point-of-view that fixing our gender gaps is going to require rethinking on every front.

Although I was happy to play the role of an outsider students could trust to ask difficult questions, my own example was viewed in China as something of a mixed bag. Mary's mother might have thought I was successful given what little she knew, but young women looking at role models like me, and ahead at their own future, didn't necessarily feel enthusiastic. Sometimes, they just felt exhausted. As one of my students pointed out, female empowerment on men's terms sometimes just seemed to present a new trap:

It may turn out that women are pushed too hard to achieve all which not only include enough femininity to attract men, good skills in nurturing children, but also strong career competence and if she fails any one of them, she would not be called a successful woman.

(This is what I see as the modern trap for women.) Many of the private conversations I held with my female colleagues, teaching assistants, friends, and students quickly turned to these kinds of personal issues.

All of my colleagues asked about my personal life,

and knew that I had managed to raise two sons, achieve the rank of tenured full professor, publish, and win some fellowships and grants. Often, they expressed doubts about how they could do all that, *if* they decided that they really wanted to. I had lots of advice for them on breaking large projects down into smaller steps that were not too overwhelming. Young academics often waste time trying to figure out a thesis, when they really should be researching an interesting question – the answer may not be apparent for months or years. They have to learn to trust the process. That's an easy one. It was harder to answer the personal questions.

At a large lecture on American censorship for faculty at GDUFS, a colleague introduced me by reading through my entire resume, extending through kudos earned twenty years earlier. At the end, he turned to me and said: "perhaps you have advice for our young women faculty who would like to accomplish all this?"

"Don't sleep," I said without thinking too much about it, as I stepped up to the podium to deliver my talk. "Just don't sleep." Everyone laughed. It was a good opening joke.

In smaller venues, I answered that common question more completely, and without the flippant edge. There were lots of common answers to making the work-family balance manageable, in both hemispheres. A supportive partner is key, as is stealing the time for writing, even if it meant ignoring your family and feeling guilty about it. I often shared the story of whining to an eminent role model in my field about the difficulty of finishing my first book. I was exhausted by the time the kids got to sleep, after teaching, driving them to lessons, cooking dinner, etc. And on the weekends, there always was house cleaning and laundry.

"I don't want to hear it," she said. "If you want to write a book, you have to write it. Stay up until midnight, work all weekend long, vacations are for writing – that's what it takes. If you aren't willing to do that, then forget about it." This tough advice came from a woman who wrote six brilliant and important books and dozens of journal articles while raising three children largely on her own. Her "you have to lose sleep" speech was the kick I needed, and a bedraggled year later, I finished.

When I tell this story (as I have dozens of times during advising sessions in Vermont), it's supposed to be inspirational. And mostly, in America, it is. With grit and determination, you can do everything! The story didn't work so well in China, for a variety of reasons. For one thing, the people I met in Guangdong province genuinely believed (not just sort of knew) that stress is bad for you. To them, my story about drinking lots of coffee to stay up late and get up early to finish my book didn't sound heroic, it sounded unhealthy. One of the frequent smirking complaints among expats was the difficulty of ever having a midday meeting. From 12:30 to 2 at GDUFS and many other places, it was naptime, and nothing could get done. Forcing yourself to stay awake with coffee sounded not just unreasonable, but also miserable and unhealthy to my Chinese friends. And for my women students, my "you can do everything with caffeine" speech also was always alien to them.

When Cheryl would complain to me about how much work she needed to do to finish her dissertation, I would say to her (with thinly veiled disgust): "Are you kidding me? You have a mother-in-law at home taking care of all the shopping, cooking, cleaning, and childcare. You have no excuse not to finish!" Essentially, this was my revised China version of the "just don't sleep" speech, delivered with exasperation bordering on intense jealousy. From my perspective, most professional mothers in China have a much better situation than the exhausted women I know in America (myself included).

Although my "just don't sleep" speech didn't go over that well in China, another mini-sermon about "making choices and allowing yourself to be imperfect" was more germane. As an example, I often described my version of Waterloo in China – trying to learn to speak Mandarin -- at which I was utterly defeated.

As soon as I received my Fulbright acceptance letter, I ordered the thick box of Rosetta Stone CDs, and began practicing several times a week. From session to session, I felt like I retained almost nothing, and by the time I arrived in China, I could say little more than "hello" and "thank you" (*nihao*, and *xie xie*), and useless things like "girls running" and "yellow car." When I asked around at GDUFS for a tutor, one of my colleagues suggested a lovely young woman who could definitely use the extra cash. She was a Chinese major, and hadn't taught foreigners before, but she was willing to try. Her name was Chelsea.

Beginning in October, Chelsea came to my apartment three times a week, and tutored me for one hour in conversational Mandarin. At first, we had some issues to work out. When I asked her if she could come at 11 in the morning, she replied "but don't you have to cook? You are a housewife!" I assured her that Emmett ate at school, and Fred and I mostly went out for lunch. She seemed shocked. The next problem was that she refused to accept any payment, insisting that it was an honor to teach me, and that was enough. Finally, with the help of a Chinese colleague, I managed to convince her that I was not the one paying – it was the United States government (which was true) – and she needed the money more than they did.

She certainly did need the money. During the course of our months of study, and sometimes meals together, Chelsea told me about her family background, coming from a

small town in Southern Guangdong province. Both of her
parents had worked at a factory, but it burned in a fire, and
since that time they had tried to eke out a living by running a
small store, which was open from 7 in the morning to 10 at
night. The family lived upstairs, and ate mostly rice, with
some fish her father caught in the South China Sea nearby.
They had no hot water, heat, or air conditioning, and from an
early age Chelsea had worked to earn some money for food
when she was not in school. Chelsea studied hard, earned a
place at GDUFS, and had been granted scholarships to help
pay the cost. She was an incredibly tough person for
someone not more than five feet tall, and probably weighing
90 pounds. I had no doubt that she was going to do well
given how hard she worked.

I am very sorry to admit that Chelsea worked a lot
harder at teaching me than I worked at learning the lessons
she prepared for me. Week after week, something else came
up. At first, it was going somewhat well, at least better than
Rosetta Stone. I learned to pronounce the sounds and tones
reasonably, so that I could read Chinese words spelled out in
"pinyin" (roman characters) and mostly be understood.
Overall, though, the situation was hopeless. In my first
semester, I was preparing three essentially new courses, and
also wrote seven different ninety-minute lectures for my
visits to other universities. Then, we had a seven-week
break, during which Chelsea went home, I started writing this
book and went on a beach vacation in the Philippines with
Fred and Emmett, and basically didn't study at all.

I will always remember a great speech given by
Marian Wright-Edelman years ago at Harvard graduation
called "Superwoman is Tired!" That's how I felt. I couldn't
teach in this new environment, manage the domestic
situation, write, and – on the side – pick up a really difficult
language with a middle-aged brain. Chelsea was thrilled to

get a fulltime job in the spring and quit her visits to our apartment – I think it was depressing to her that I was such a pathetic student, and that all her hard work and carefully-written lesson plans went to waste.

When I think about the range of women I came to know in China, it reminds me that just as in the United States, we are rarely superheroes, and manage only to do some things well, but never everything. And it is never useful to lump women with lots of choices, like Alice, in with those who have far fewer, like Chelsea, whether in America or in China. Global, bullet-point statistics never tell the whole story. As many critics have pointed out, the writings of Betty Friedan and Helen Gurley Brown were essentially useless for the millions of poor women who never had the option not to work, or the free time to enjoy (safe) sexy, "thrilling affairs." Chelsea is definitely in that camp, and thankfully has a brighter future because of China's relatively meritocratic education system. If economic growth continues, she will be able to raise her own child in far greater comfort, and probably lift her parents from poverty as well.

In Alice's case, she ended up getting her son back in the spring. She gave up one of her teaching jobs to have some more time at home, which made her parents feel better about the situation, but she was still planning to finish her PhD. I'd like to think that perhaps Cheryl and I played a small part in convincing her that she had every right to insist on raising her own son (sisterhood is powerful). Either way, I was happy to see her and her husband beaming before I left, rushing off as always in a hurry, but happy and complete. They are saving up the money to pay the fine and have another child within the next few years. Cheryl also hopes the one-child policy will be revised; there have been proposals in China to allow two parents who are both only children to have a second, in which case she also wants to have another – and this time, they both hope for a girl.

Conclusion. Education Matters

The last two weeks of our stay in Guangzhou sped by in a blur. Many colleagues and friends wanted to host us for lavish farewell lunches and dinners, at which we often were presented with thoughtful and sometimes expensive parting gifts – a Swarovski pendant, silk scarves, framed calligraphy, boxed sets of fancy pens, etc. As at all of the formal meals I attended in China, each event began with a host ushering me to the *feng shui* seat of honor, facing the door, flanked by the first and second most senior people in the room. There were lots of formal photographs of handshakes and gift exchanges. Waitresses would begin loading up the Lazy Susan as soon as everyone sat down, but nobody touched the food until the host made an opening toast. I was used to all of this by the end of June, but even so I was impressed and somewhat overwhelmed; my Chinese colleagues were exquisitely good at saying goodbye.

One farewell dinner, though, was more strange and humorous than anything else, especially because I had never met the host. It was a dinner arranged by Graham's boss, or I should say, *one* of Graham's bosses. Right from the beginning of our trip in China, he was besieged by parents who wanted him to tutor their children in English. This wasn't anything he had intended to do; in fact, Graham hoped more than anything else to spend the year perfecting his Chinese, and living as much as possible "as the Romans do."

Graham's desire to live anonymously on the streets of Guangzhou, however, proved difficult. Instead, his pale skin, blue eyes, dark plastic glasses, and brown hair often attracted a crowd. When we would walk in downtown parks and tourist attractions, flocks of young Chinese boys and girls would run up to him yelling "Harry Potter!" and insist on having their photo taken with him. He also received a variety of relatively lucrative, though sometimes bizarre, job offers. Once, he got paid the equivalent of $100 to stand on stage at a corporate event and speak one line of English – presumably to impress the guests with the company's foreign connections.

Graham also accepted several tutoring jobs, including a private company that charged parents exorbitant fees for the privilege of their child attending "class" taught by an 18-year old American with no teaching experience or curricular materials. He mostly sang songs with the small children in his charge, and tried to keep them from climbing on the table. Another man living near our campus hired him to tutor his teenage son. Graham asked if the father wanted him to work on conversation skills and he scoffed – "I don't care if he can speak English, I just want him to do well on the high school test!"

Although Graham was frustrated with his tutoring jobs in general, he was happy to accept the cash. Over the course of the year, he continued to accept reasonable offers, including one from a very persistent father he met on the Guangzhou metro in early spring. Thankfully, Mr. Wei turned out to be a lovely man, and for several months in the spring, he paid handsomely for regular tutoring, and Graham got to know the family fairly well.

Mr. Wei and his family had moved to Guangzhou from a village in Jiangxi province. His wife had gained admission to a Guangdong medical school, and her skills were valuable, so they had been able to obtain the precious *hukou* permit that allowed them to buy property and enroll their son in school in Guangzhou. Of course, grandma and other relatives had come along as well. Now, the family was fairly prosperous, with funds earned from building and renting small apartment complexes in a suburban area of the city.

Mr. Wei approached Graham because he has one sincere, intense, even obsessive wish for the future -- that his son "Sean" attends college at Harvard. He talked about this with Graham incessantly, hoping that the English tutoring would help the cause. Bemused by Mr. Wei's insistence, Graham mentioned that I had graduated from Harvard, and so knew a lot about it firsthand. After that, Mr. Wei wouldn't leave Graham alone about the idea of having Sean meet me. I sent some Harvard pencils, a key chain and shirt for Sean, but none of that was enough. Mr. Wei wanted his son to "shake hands" with a Harvard graduate and therefore "be inspired" to study hard enough to get in. Finally, with just days to go before our departure, we scheduled a dinner so that Sean could meet me. Mr. Wei brought his shiny new Volvo to the gates of GDUFS on a warm evening, and drove Graham, his girlfriend Meimei, and me to a restaurant near the apartment complexes he had built and managed.

To our surprise, the private dining room was packed when we arrived. Sean's mother was there, as well as Mr. Wei's business partners and elderly relatives, who all came from the same village. The feast was lavish, with enormous prawns, delicate soft tofu, braised lotus root, and steamed whole fish. I finally ate some foods I truly had been dreading – turtle (pets, not meat!), and snake (too many bones for my taste). Throughout the strange evening, the conversation kept returning to Harvard – not what it was like or what I studied there, but only how to get in. "Sean should keep reading a great deal," I offered via Meimei, as my ace translator. "Harvard students are great readers." "Oh he reads all the time!" his mother proudly boasted. The conversation went on like that for a long time.

I wasn't terribly surprised about the Harvard obsession, or even by the fact that the Wei family didn't seem to care at all where it was, or what kind of education Sean would receive if he were admitted. By the end of June, I had seen a lot of that from the general public. The name was all that mattered – Harvard has really good face in China.

Although Sean probably will never be accepted to Harvard, he almost certainly will go to college somewhere in the United States. In April, the *International Business Times* reported on a study of Chinese "luxury consumers" which found that 85% of Chinese with more than one million US dollars in assets intended to send their children abroad for education, with America the number one destination. The attraction is not frivolous. Fourteen of the top twenty universities in the world, according to 2012 rankings, are in the United States. Our higher education system is universally acknowledged as the best in the world. Among the reasons cited were our "cross-disciplinary fields and development of critical thinking." Peking University, China's flagship, came in at forty-ninth.

I thought about this a lot when I came back to Saint Michael's in September, and began my annual fall ritual of teaching seminars for first-year students. Although the title of the course I have developed for them is "Looking at Art," I am very clear from the start that art is a sideshow to the major purpose of the course, which is to teach first-year students the critical thinking and communications skills they need "for success in college and beyond." For fourteen weeks, I will hound them to interrogate everything they look at and read, and to develop and articulate their own informed, thoughtful, and critical contributions to our conversations. I will force them to do such strange and difficult things as writing an in-depth formal analysis of an object in their dorm room. (Past subjects have included a leopard-skin patterned bra, a Ping-Pong table made of beer bottle caps, and an iron that "came out of the closet" with its owner.) My students may not like such wacky assignments, but they will stretch their capacity for insight, analysis, and creativity -- which are powerful building blocks for innovation. Teaching creativity is the toughest challenge of all, and it doesn't come cheap. I will log hundreds of hours this semester meeting with each of my thirty students individually, commenting extensively on their essays, demanding re-writes, and pushing them to challenge their assumptions and think in new ways.

At the same time I returned to Saint Michael's ready to frustrate, expand, and hopefully inspire first-year students again, I also encountered an intensified firestorm of doomsday prognostications about the future of my craft. If recent journal articles, think-tank papers, and online screeds are to be believed, then face-to-face teaching like my small seminar is doomed, thanks to the challenges of economic downturn, decreased government funding for colleges and students, and the opportunities presented by the Internet. MOOCs – Massive Open Online Courses offered for free by the bigwigs at Stanford, Princeton, MIT, etc., are expected to make classes taught by lesser mortals like myself unnecessary. Standardized, computer-graded assessments will allow students around the world to demonstrate their proficiency at little cost. And "accountability" experts (vocalizing especially loudly at election time) promise that such computerized tests can eliminate the variability and squishiness of the American academic experience. These experts probably would not be impressed by the first-year seminar I teach: my students will not take a single exam during the semester, nor gain a shred of directly applicable work experience that could feed a resume.

This all is bitter irony indeed, since many of

America's conservative educational reformers are trying to remake our system in the image of China's (cheap and standardized), at the same time that practically everyone in China with the means to do so is trying to get their kid into a classroom like mine. It is no accident that most of the world's most important and lucrative 21st century innovations (for example the laptop and smart phone) are the product of individuals educated in America's "unaccountable" and relatively freewheeling schools and universities.

Each of our countries has an educational system rooted in its past, that was developed long ago to support its particular societal structure. In China, the ancient system of high-stakes testing fed students into a hierarchy with little room for mobility; your score on an exam was an efficient reminder of where you stood in the social order, and few qualified for significant instruction. That's still true today.

In America, Benjamin Franklin was in the forefront of those who recognized that democracy would require broad public education. Our masses were not principally laborers in a feudal system – instead, their combined intellects and talents would determine the fate of the nation. The subjects taught at first were quite limited, but after the Civil War, federal, state, and local legislatures invested significant tax funds to create a vast network of public universities with a large number of disciplinary majors. The Servicemen's Readjustment Act of 1944 (a.k.a. "G. I. Bill") and Fulbright program were natural federal investments following ample successful precedent. Relative academic freedom, and faculty empowered to experiment through the benefits of tenure, combined to produce remarkable progress in the craft of teaching young adults. American taxpayers got their money's worth on all counts; because of our system of higher education and the inventiveness it spawned, we became the intellectual envy of the world.

The Chinese academics I met were well aware of the connection between our first-class colleges and universities, innovation skills, and economic growth, and all expected their own system to gradually evolve to look more like ours. They knew this wouldn't be fast or easy, but nonetheless they peppered me with questions about how we teach critical thinking, and insisted that I run my classrooms in China just as I did at home – in order to "broaden the horizons" of my students. Five-year plans issued by the Ministry of Education all emphasize the need to adopt more interactive Western-style teaching in order to build a workforce that can compete in the global 21st century.

These realities and realizations made American conversations about decreased funding; increased standardized testing, massive online education; and the death of liberal arts curricula seem reckless when I got back home. Federal and state governments seemed bent on continuing to withdraw their support from higher education, even though the result is skyrocketing student debt, plummeting social mobility, and a bleak prognosis for our continued economic predominance. The scathing rhetoric today on higher education sometimes spins out as though our 20th-century successes were entirely unrelated to government investments. History lessons to the contrary are desperately in order.

The lessons of China's example made these conversations seem even more egregious to me than they naturally had before my year abroad. How pathetic that we would consider devolving a higher education system that is the envy of the world, and that has been an economic driver for our prosperity. And how doubly pathetic, if we care at all about foreign affairs, that we would consider diminishing our most important soft power. As the world's leader in higher education, we welcome future leaders from around the globe to our shores, thus building invaluable fraternal and sororal bonds for the future of our diplomatic efforts.

Some of the fault undoubtedly is our own within "the academy." One of the more embarrassing questions I had to answer in China came from Chinese Fulbrighters who had gone to America for study and/ or teaching. "Why do the students drink so much and smoke marijuana?" they commonly asked me. And "why do Americans have so many guns?" I met several Chinese students who were afraid to come to the United States, thinking that there were snipers on every corner.

Coming back to America was, indeed, a wake up call. At my first-year advising session the weekend before classes, one young man looked so stoned I thought he would fall out of his chair. Later, I heard that after the pomp and circumstance of our formal welcome ceremony, orientation leaders were giving water bottles filled with cheap tequila to the new students, as a "proper" welcome to their new home. Saint Michael's, of course, is not alone in battling student alcohol abuse. In contrast, I never had to remind any of my Chinese students about the purpose of their education, and although there is no drinking age in China, I rarely had to reckon with students in class who looked like they were recovering from 'a few too many' the night before. In China, most of the students have a Mr. Wei at home.

My conversations with Chinese colleagues on the differences between higher education in our two countries always would end with the same assessment: a perfect university would provide the benefits of both systems. Students and the nation could reach their intellectual, creative, and economic potential through educational institutions that combined the opportunity for social mobility through a "fair," meritocratic, and affordable system; a rigorous workload requiring disciplined work habits; and creative instruction and the freedom to take risks in speaking, publishing, teaching, and learning without fear of punishment. To be fair, many of my own students achieve this ideal already, by working hard and taking advantage of the best professors and resources at Saint Michael's and abroad. In America's elite universities, the proportion of students achieving this goal undoubtedly already is extremely high, as it was when I attended Harvard twenty-five years ago.

But honestly, far too many American young people squander the opportunities they are given. The beautiful, earnest, and hard-working Chinese students I met also were a varied crew, but overall there really wasn't much comparison. Huge weight sat on their shoulders -- to achieve, and to succeed, not only for their own futures, but also for those of the parents and grandparents who will depend on them. Our students in America could use a lot more gravitas – college education is often seen as a middle-class birthright here, when it should be seen as a privilege earned through sustained and unremitting effort.

After dinner with the Wei family I felt sorry for poor Sean. Here was a skinny little twelve-year old with big glasses hanging off his nose, surrounded by grown-ups who pinned their hopes on his narrow shoulders, to permanently elevate the status of the entire family (maybe their entire village in Jiangxi province) through admission to a college in America they had never even seen pictures of. He seemed completely uninterested in the conversation going on around him. But he was listening, and the desperate insistence that he achieve extraordinary success will only grow louder as he enters high school, and prepares for the *gaokao* and SAT exams that will determine his fate, and his family's face.

My hope for Sean, and for all my friends in China, is that they will grow wiser and stronger in a country that gradually (and soon) grants them more freedom, empowerment, safety, and health. To all those in America who say that we can't afford the work of the EPA, OSHA, and other regulatory bodies in our government, I say – go live in China for a year. You might just be surprised by the lessons you bring home. I feel almost guilty each day when our beautiful Vermont sky is crystal clear, and the water from the tap is not merely drinkable without boiling, but clean and refreshing

My hope for America is that we wake up to the realities of our place in the world, and to the importance of education in maintaining our lofty stature. America is not an exceptional country as that phrase is used in contemporary politics, but we still enjoy exceptional prestige as the nation most associated with what "equality," "liberty," "development," "modernity," and "academic excellence" are supposed to look like.

In 1966, J. William Fulbright wrote that "If America has a service to perform in the world and I believe it has, it is in large part the service of its own example . . . Most of all, we have the opportunity to serve as an example of democracy to the world by the way in which we run our own society." Clearly, he believed that the examples of our higher education system, and our democratic way of life, were the most powerful tools we have for positively changing troubled spheres of the globe. I agree.

Fulbright is by no means a perfect historical figure viewed through a liberal, post-modern prism. He battled against McCarthyism and the House Un-American Activities Committee, but he also supported segregation, and believed that only soft power, and not military intervention, should be used in combatting overseas horrors. But in America, as I taught my students, we are adept at reconciling the complex realities of our historical past and its imperfect heroes. Fulbright's legacy should still be admired, "warts and all."

There is no mystery as to why he was the man who most fully recognized the powerful role and example of American higher education in the world. He was elected to the House of Representatives after several years of service as President of the University of Arkansas at Fayetteville – a product of federal, state, and county investment in higher education made possible by the Morrill Act of 1862 (a piece of legislation sponsored by one of Vermont's foremost federal legislators). Those were the days when Americans looked to their future with great expectations. Their investment in higher education paid off handsomely. One of the lessons I have taken home from China is that the historical example of that period is still relevant. Education is still the key to our future, even more so than ever before. Our leaders and citizens should wake up to that reality and act accordingly, before we blow our lead in the game.

Personally, I intend to earn my keep as a professor going forward by teaching with an invigorated sense of the excellence, and importance, of what happens on my campus. I brought home more literally sobering lessons as well. In my classroom this semester, I intend to be tougher on my students than I have been before. They face stiff competition in their future, and they need to understand just how many incredibly hard-working students around the world are aiming their sights at the privileges we enjoy.

No singular conclusion could adequately summarize the lessons from China that I absorbed during my year in Guangzhou, but one powerful idea does rise to the top of that long list: America and China have much to learn from each other, and from history, if we are to achieve the best possible versions of our future selves. I hope that back in China, the faculty and students I worked with gleaned some clear lessons from America as well. *Xie xie* to my dear friends, colleagues, and students in China, to my valiant Fulbright colleagues, and to all of us who labor in the invigorating work of higher education around the world. Our past is our best guide to the future in which we are, irrevocably, intertwined.